FIRST EDITION-
Published in the United States of America. (U.S).
By CreateSpace an Amazon Company.

ISBN-13: 978-1502470133

ISBN-10: 1502470136

DEDICATION.

To God Almighty, To my Family & Friends, To All my Mentors and To You, my Readers all Around the World.
Readers are Thinkers, Thinkers are Leaders and Deep Thinkers are Great Leaders. The Reading Habit is a Rich Habit. The Rich Read.

ACKNOWLEDGEMENT .

I am Grateful to God Almighty, for the grace to start and complete this book at the right time, through thick and thin.
To My mentors who have contributed their quota to humanity and added value to human existence.

FOREWORD.

Debt is the Money from the Poor and Wealth is the Money of the Rich. They Lied, that "Money is the Root of all Evil". No! "The Love of Money Is the Root of all Evil and the Lack of Money Motivates Evil Actions". Poverty is not the lack of money or state of being broke. Poverty is a state of mind. According to history, we know that poverty is the root cause of crime and corruption in the World today, and only if the government can wake up to their responsibilities, to fight poverty in the World, crime and corruption will be drastically reduced.

Success can Happen to Anyone Who Desires to be Successful, at any location anywhere in the World. Anyone can become successful in life. J.K Rowling a Mentor, Writer, Author and Creator of the Harry Potter Collection, stumbled on an idea to write books for kids, that idea turned out to be a multi-billion dollar Empire. While she was waiting on a delayed train from Manchester to London, then a depressed young lady. She is now a Self-Made Billionaire Bestselling Author.
Selling over 500 million books Worldwide of the World Famous Harry Potter Series.

Premeditated Success Precedes Good Success in Any Endeavor your Heart Desires in Life. Wealth Creation must be premeditated if you must be Rich and Wealthy in life. There is a course of action or action plan to success and prosperity. It's more about Taking Action towards your Goals and Targets than having Wild Dreams. You have to start by Developing a Rich Mindset. Wealth Creation Begins With a Wealth Mentality and Wisdom is the Fundamental Principle for Wealth Creation, With a Heart Desire for Abundance and Prosperity, Napoleon Hill calls it a "Burning Desire" in his book "Think and Grow Rich". People are Made to Believe That Money is a Scarce Resource, and this lie becomes unconsciously programed in their minds and invariably forms their Mind set, Affects their Lifestyle and Limits their means of Livelihood and Financial Status. The Simple Reason for the Limitations of Money and the Shortage of Cash People Experience from Time to Time , is due to Scarcity Mentality they have unconsciously built and Programed in their Minds. This Book will prepare you for Million Dollar and Billion Dollar Net Worth. However, If your purpose and intentions are only financially motivated, then you will be working for Money, this is not wrong though, but If your Purpose and Intentions are Value Motivated and Value Driven, Money Will Work for You.

It's Possible to be Living in the Midst of Opportunities and Still Be poor. You can be Surrounded by Riches, and Still be Impoverished. You Can be Walking on a Treasure Land and Not Be Aware , You can be standing on a Gold Mine and Not Notice, You can be Sitting in a Box of Fortune and Not Be Conscious, and You can be Living on an Oil Field and Not be Aware. You Might have what is takes to be a Billionaire and Remain Poor. Your Self Worth Determines Your Network and your Network determines your Net Worth. Prosperity is the proof of Success. You can not Fantasize or Wish for Cash to Get Rich in life, You have to Properly Prepare yourself for Wealth Creation and Practically Practice the Principles of Wealth Creation to Prevent being poor in life because No one prepares for Battle on the Battlefield, if they must win . Whenever there is Scarcity anywhere, Abundance is always available elsewhere. Your hundred mile journey to success, starts with a step in the right direction to enable you to save time and enhance your arrival at your desired successful destination.

Money will be the last thing you will live to never worry about again in your life after reading this book. You are not to serve or Work for Money, Money is working for you and Serve you. Money Matters, but Money is not your Master, you are the Master of Money. Money answers all things, but money is not everything with respect to health and long life. In this book, you will discover how to develop a Rich Mind. I call it the "Gold Mind". Starting from the Seed of Inspiration, Words, Knowledge, Thoughts, Revelations, Imagination, Creativity, Insights, Dreams , Visions and Ideas (conception) through the Time of Growth (nurture), to the time of Reality or the Season of Harvest (maturity). You will DISCOVER how money will work for you and you can stop working for money.   One percent Rich faith is all you need to solve Ninety Nine financial problems. "Money Works".

Success can Happen Anywhere in the World to Anyone Who Desires to be Successful, the Principles in this book are Universal. You will discover the Mastery of Money. Money is a means to an end and a medium of Exchange. We determine the value of the Cash we Make, Save, Spend and Invest. The Dollar bills, Banknotes and Currency in your bank account is of no value till the worth is ascertain and evaluated. Your Net worth is a measure of your Wealth and Asset against your liabilities. If you are living on credit, you are poor. If your credit is more than your Income and Earning, you are poor.

You may look rich though, but you are not rich at all because your liabilities are beyond your assets. The house, cars and other properties you have are not assets, they are liabilities, because you acquired them on credit and they keep you in debt. You will have to outlive your debt, You need multiple streams of income, you need residual income, you will have to earn more money. You have to start trading with your gift, talent, skills, knowledge and expertise. You don't want to write a Will of debt for your kids or die poor. This book will teach you Debt management , Wealth Management, Risk Management, Resource Management and Resource Control.

In This book you will discover how to get out of Debt and start Living Rich. Lots of Countries, Organizations, Corporations, Companies , Families and Individuals in the World today are in debt, but that can change. You can Move from Debt to Wealth and Advance From Financial Crisis to Financial Stability.

Third World countries are poverty stricken because their citizens live below one dollar per day, that's why they are called poor countries, they have a poor standard of living and have low Per-Capita-Income , low GDP and GNI. Advanced countries are Indebted because the majority of their Citizens live on Credit, they are unemployed with the bad state of the economy and bad economic condition because they consume more than they produce, creating a situation where, there is minimal resource availability for so many people. We will be astonished to know, that most of the Third World countries especially Africa, have immense wealth of natural resources like Human capital, Energy, Crude Oil, Natural Gas, Gold, Diamond, Steel, Iron Ore, Lime Stone, Coal, Silicon, Bitumen, Bauxite and other Food and Cash crops, But their problem is developing, managing and controlling these resources, thats why they are poor. You will be shocked to find out that the Value of the Natural resources in some Third World countries, is Worth all the Money in the World put together.

You may find yourself in that same situation, when you don't Discover, Develop and Display your Gifts,Talent, Skills and Expertise. Anything of Value you possess, but you don't use, will become useless, no matter how valuable it is to you, most especially Information. If you know better, you will do better. If you are not informed, you will be deformed. Knowledge is light and knowledge can become powerful, if you act on it, but Knowledge is not enough, you may know it all and still be Disadvantaged. Wisdom is much more Important, because Wisdom is the correct application of knowledge. Wisdom is acting on the knowledge you have. "Act on it". If you have money tied down anywhere, it's not going to increase or reproduce itself. You need to make your money work for you, by investing in yourself to develop your skills, expertise and talent or by investing money in profitable ventures and You can better save up for Investment Purposes.

Wisdom is the Principal thing, Therefore get Wisdom and Wisdom is Profitable to Direct. A word is enough for the Wise. The onus is on you to discover where your passion lies, then explore it, develop it, and display it, Act on it, Trade with it and use it to add value and affect lives positively. Don't quench your quest for Finance , this is the best time to be Financially Stable.

AUTHOR'S QUOTES:- Anyone Can Get Rich but Not Everyone Can Stay Rich, because Money is a Temporary Visitor, Money is not a Permanent Friend . In Money Book you will discover the Mastery of Money and how Prudence Matters to Money. You will also Discover the difference between Wealth and Riches.

CONTENTS-

Author's Note...

-       Stranded at the train station in the wee hours of the night, on a trip from New Your City to Los Angeles, She was all alone by herself as she looked around, and it seems she was not going to make it to L.A same day. She got furious and frustrated. She needed a means of escape and an urgent way out of her misery. She had no cash on her, as all the banks were closed at that time of the day . She made several phone calls for rescue, but all hope seems to be lost, her phone battery was dying. Feeling lonely at the train station, she became nervous and anxious. Her life is at risk and her bags may soon disappear as the footfall of strangers increased in the walkway. She had better make the last call now, or else her phone will shut down and she will spend the rest of the night at the train station with no working cell phone.

Then, she thought to herself on the way forward. Deep down within, she knew that fear will cause her more harm, and being nervous and anxious will be detrimental to her progress at that moment. She knew she had better stop fretting and start thinking. This new thought process, suppressed her anxiety and worries, and she was able to stabilize her emotions and mindset. Then clarity came, she figured out what to do, and that was the solution to her journey to get to her destination. She has only one chance to make the most vital phone call for the best possible solution. She made a distance call to an old friend. Narrating the ordeal of her journey so far. Her friend suggested to her on the best way to help, will be, for him to send money to her via mobile money transfer.   He agreed to help her out, few seconds after their phone conversation, he stepped out to the closest store in the neighborhood, a couple of blocks from his home, to purchase a Money Card, in the amount she needs, in the cash value. He opened up the panel on the card covering the money card pin code of number digits. He sent the number pin code via text message to her and she was able to load the pin on her ATM card through her bank account. The Money Reflected instantly in her bank account as the exact cash value of the card purchased used on her ATM card. That was the rescue mission, for her journey to her destination.

She instantly purchased the smart pass necessary to get on board the last available Train to Los Angeles, California. It could have been a job interview or an emergency. Desperate times calls for desperate measures. Never worry, fret, nervous or anxious, in any situation, it will cause you more harm than good and can lead to uncontrollable disaster. You can never get anything right under anxiety. You will make lots of mistakes. Mistakes can be very costly, we will examine that later in this book. It has been discovered that people, have lost valuable possessions, ideas, their minds and even their lives, all because of anxiety and worry. Depression is as a result of anxiety and worry. Be anxious for Nothing. When you get anxious, you lose your mind temporarily. You stop thinking and you start sinking like the Titanic. Worry will never stop the challenges of tomorrow, it will only drain you of the strength available today. Stop Worrying and Start Thinking, Start Thinking and Start Living.

-Signed by The Author.

INTRODUCTION.-

You can get an Education in Schools, You can be taught Success in Relationships, You can be groomed to attain any position in life, You can learn professional skills to do better at your job, You can be trained to achieve a better career, You can get successful marriage counseling, You can be Advised on Business and Leadership Success , You can be Taught how to be a law abiding citizen to your country, but No one will Teach you how to Make Money and Stay Rich in Life, The Good news for you today is, that Money Book is here to the Rescue.

In case you don't know, the truth is "Money is Everywhere Around you in form of Opportunities and Wealth is Your Ability to Identify, Recognize and Discover these Opportunities, and turn the Opportunities to Cash Flow. Anyone can get Rich, but not everyone can Stay Rich.

It's Possible to be Living in the midst of Opportunities and be Poor. Wealth is not only available below our feet as natural resources, but also inside us as Gifts, Talents, Abilities, Potentials, Inspiration and Skills and around us as opportunities and ideas. Poverty is not the Absence or Lack of Money, Poverty is a State of Mind. Latest study show, that over $10 Trillion Dollars worth of Natural Resources is under our feet, from crude oil to natural gas, gold, diamonds, steel, iron ore, coal, limestone, bitumen, bauxite, silicon.

Now, imagine the world of human resources, available in humans as potentials, worthy of development, to help harness the available natural resources available under our feet in the Earth Crust.

After studying Money Book, you will advance from Debt to WEALTH and move from the Financial Crisis to Financial Freedom. You Will Discover how to get rich & live wealthy. You will become Financially Free.

Money Book is about Staying Rich, and Staying Rich is about the Mastery of Money and Money Mastery means Financial Independence.
You will Stop Working for Money, Money will Start Working for You and You will Understand how "Money Works". You will find out what the Rich Know about Money, that keeps them wealthy. Anyone can get Rich, but not everyone can Stay Rich, but the Utmost Desire of my heart is for you to get rich and wealthy, prosperous and live longer, just as the longing of your soul.   Wealth is, making money work for you and stay with you". You will discover the difference between being Rich, and being Wealthy. Money Book Is About Turning Opportunities to Cash Flow.

WEALTH METAMORPHOSIS-

Think Rich for Financial Freedom & Live Wealthy.

The Truth about Money is that Money is a temporary visitor, Money is not a permanent friend. That is where prudence comes in. People are asking , Where the Money at? The truth is Money is around you littered everywhere in form of opportunities. Not a single currency note or coin disappeared, ever since the invention and creation of Money and Currencies. Money is neither a permanent friend nor a permanent Visitor. Money can visit anyone at anytime and can leave anytime. To make money your permanent friend and visitor then you must be Prudent with what you do with money. Money sometimes grows wings, and can fly. Opportunities are invisible Money as potentials everywhere around us, and inside us as talents, around us as ideas. The ability to unlock, decode and convert these opportunities to real value and cash flow is Wealth Creation, then You can make money visit you every time and stay with you forever.

Napoleon Hill in his book "Think and Grow Rich" talked about Paradigm Shift, What Paradigm shift means is simply the movement of wealth and resources from one hand that holds it down to another hand that needs it. The Global Financial Crisis is simply a Paradigm Shift. You have to position yourself for Wealth Creation. In every disadvantage, there is always an advantage, For every casting down, there is always a lifting up, For every setback there is always a stepping stone.

Financial crisis happens, to give room for Wealth Creation. Money and Wealth Creation are changing Hands in the World today, where some Countries in the World, that use to be poor 20 years ago are now lending money to rich Countries. "Your setback is a setup for your comeback".

CHAPTER 1.

The Best Ivy League and Business Schools in the World might teach you everything you need to know about Business and Finance but they will never teach you how to Think Rich for financial freedom and how you can ultimately Get Rich and Stay Rich, also the richest people in the World will not tell you their success and trade secrets, but this book Will. Knowledge is not Enough, Wisdom is the Principal Thing. This Book will teach you Wisdom and Understanding.

14 years ago as the captain of the High School Basketball Team. I told my teammates that, our mind is the battlefield of our lives, where we win or lose the games of life. You can't prepare for a battle on the battlefield if you must win. Sometime ago at a public lecture, I told my audience that "Your mind is the Treasure land of your life where you plant seeds of words, thoughts, dreams, ideas, creativity, imaginations, revelations, knowledge, visions, possibilities, greatness and desires, and you reap the harvest of wealth, riches, abundance, fame, fortune, peace of mind, happiness, long life and blessings. Today I am a living proof of my own words. Also we can plant seeds of fear, doubts, procrastinations, defeat, laziness, ignorance, foolishness and negativity and harvest poverty, lack, want and defeat. What is fear, if I may ask. Fear is the unreal uncertainties, we paint in our mind that keeps us in bondage and oppression for as long as we permit it. And What is faith? Faith is not the absence of fear, but believing and pressing on, in the face of defeat, depression, challenges and uncertain, situations. Either you Win or you lose, either your situation is Good or bad, it's all your Choice and your Decision, because you are the Architect of your own life, The captain of your own soul and the leader and ruler of your own destiny. You choose and decide the quality of your own life.

Any situation or circumstance can happen to anyone at anytime, but it's up to you to make the situation temporary or permanent. It's your choice to make that situation remain with you for life or for a moment.

Often times in life, we face temporary defeat or we are overtaken by temporary setbacks, but it's up to us to decide if we choose to remain in that situation, or take the bull by the horn, stand our ground and face that situation head on and conquer it and Promise ourself never to quit and give up till we overcome and conquer. You are the Captain of your own soul, The Architect of your own Life and The Ruler of your own Destiny". You need to take responsibilities for your own life. Good or Bad, No Excuse for failure. It's very normal for People to sit back and blame everyone else for their short comings. "Oh, My father was the reason. "If only, I can Travel Abroad. "Oh, Why didn't my mum know better. "Oh, It's the Government". "Oh The Leaders are not Responsible enough" Oh, why didn't he go to school. "If you know better, you will do better". Ignorance is no excuse in life.

THINK AHEAD, STAY AHEAD -

Think Ahead, Stay Ahead, Be at the Top of Your Game.
We all have the ability to THINK, even if you think you have nothing to think about or you have got no skill or talent. It all starts with a thought in your heart to spark the change in your life. We can all think of anything we desire, and that Opens Our Mind to the World of endless Possibilities, Insights, Creativity, Ideas, Dreams, Visions, and Imaginations. One thought is all you need to make a great difference in your life. You are one thought

away to become as rich as you have ever imagined and beyond your Widest Dreams.

Thoughts are Seeds and can come in the form of ideas. The School of thought is opened to everyone and you need no permission or application to gain admission and access. It's opened to all that desire to Think.

Our lives is greatly influenced by our thoughts. Since the beginning of time,

we have done things differently in the World, because people dared to think differently. Great works have been witnessed in our time because people decided to Think differently.

Great works are results of Deep thoughts. To be great in life, you must be a deep Thinker. Thinkers are Leaders and Deep Thinkers are Great Leaders. You can't be a deep thinker and not become a great leader. Thoughts lights up the ideas in our minds. Your mental picture is your real future.
We all do things in certain ways because of our own thoughts. We do different things in the World today because some people chose to think differently. The course of life has been changed from time to time in different areas because some people dared to Think Deep . You can't lead, if you are not a thinker, thinking spurs you to lead. The more you think deep the better you lead. Give to positive thinking, its the light of your Soul. If You Think Deep, you will rise high in life.

The Rich Think Rich, so the Middle Class Think Average and the Poor Think Poor. It's all in your Thought Process. If you Think like the Rich, you will do what the Rich do and you will eventually become Rich, same way, if you think average you will do what the middle class do and you will eventually remain middle class, If you think poor, you will do what poor people do and you will eventually become poor. The difference between the rich and the poor is how they Think, or their mind-set. You are what you think. The poor man's idea is useless to the rich simply because he thinks poor. Your thoughts do not really determine your looks, but greatly influence how you talk.The easiest way people determine who you are is by what you say, which is a proof of your thought process or thinking pattern. Your Talk is the Reflection of your Thought. By their fruits, you will know them, as the saying goes.

If you Think like a Millionaire, you will Do what Millionaires do, and you will eventually become a Millionaire. If you Think like a Billionaire, you will do what Billionaires Do and you will eventually become a Billionaire. Same way, If you Think like the middle class, you will do what the middle class do and eventually remain middle class, if you think like the poor, you will do what poor people do and you will eventually become poor. No one ever wants to be poor, but let me tell you why people are poor. The simple reason is because, they unconsciously do things that makes people poor. Poor mindset, poverty mentality, Poor Knowledge, indolence, slothfulness, procrastination, laziness, arrogance, fear of failure, disbelieve and hopelessness, lack of faith, needy and beggarly lifestyle, misery, problems and defeat mentality. How do the Rich Think? They Think Rich- They have a positive and Rich Mindset, They take Bold Steps, They take Risks, They Develop Self Confidence , they are strong, they have good courage, they are brave, they have faith and, they believe, they are hopeful, they are focused, they have the Winning Attitude, positive mentality, abundance mentality, generosity and empathy.

They Think Rich, They Talk Rich, They Act Rich and They Live Rich. As a public speaker, I tell people that the easiest and best way to know how people think is when you hear them talk. Then you will know their thought quality or their stinking thinking.

CHAPTER 2-

THINK OUTSIDE THE BOX & STEP OUT-

Don't be confined or limited to the conventional way people think, think differently, think better, think of solutions, think of improvements, think of progress, think of better ways of doing things. Think Rich!. If the rich can Think Rich, so can You. The advent of technology has made life easier and results are achieved better these days. Don't be the tool, use the tool. Result these days are achieved better, faster and easier. Take advantage of Information Technology for Wealth Creation. Don't conform yourself to the ordinary and common lifestyle, transform your lifestyle by renewing your mind. It's crucial to moving up to your next level and you step up in life. Take calculated Risk.

REBRAND-

Consumers are enlightened and more tech-savvy, thus Rebranding may be your game changer. You may have to change the way you package and present your brand for a new market appeal. People buy the brand first before buying what you are offering for sale, meaning people accept your brand first before listening to what you have to offer. The marketplace is not about who is right or wrong, it's about who is successful.There are lots of competitors in the same market , but each market place always has the leading product or the market leader. Rebranding, may also have to be, changing your sale strategy, or changing your marketing tactics. Your sales approach or sales pitch may be what you need to get right. You can be selling the right product in the wrong market and you can be selling the wrong product in the right market.

Sell the right product in the right market. Carve your niche and stay ahead of your competitors. Think of better ways of getting into the heart of the customers and how your brand can last long in the mind of the consumers. Make your brand stand out in the Marketplace and be known for your uniqueness. Create Innovative concepts that will make your brand memorable. Think deeply on fresh insights and your outcome and results will be outstanding. Identify your Niche Market , Reach out to the right Demography and your Unique selling point. What are the features that make your brand appealing to the consumers ?

Network Marketing and New Media like Online Marketing , Social Media Marketing, Mobile and Digital Marketing & Advertising, Blogging , Tweets, Viral Pictures, Videos & messages, Innovative and Insightful Concepts-

These days, Consumers are more informed and enlightened about New Media Markrting, they want more value for their money, consumers want to pay less to derive more satisfaction for spending on anything, and the solution for the 21st century business is Network Marketing. In the next few years to come, Trade, Import and Export will be determined by Network Marketing. I believe the Government and Organizations of every country in the World should start investing very well in Network Marketing as the solution to the Economic Meltdown. They should encourage Citizens, Families and Individuals start using Word of Mouth to Promote goods and Services locally produced in their countries.
Local content should be encouraged, in every country of the World, if they must move from Debt to Wealth, from the Financial Crisis to Financial Stability, this will boost IGR (Internally Generated Revenue) and Boost International Trade for competitive advantage. In a situation where comparative advantage comes in then network marketing should be used as the tool to drive sales.

CROWD FUNDING, VENTURE CAPITAL & MICRO FINANCE.

Over the last few years, a myriad of online platforms for lending money, funding projects and sourcing information have popped up across the Internet. With so many surface similarities, it's easy to see why you might get a little confused.

Is Kiva a crowfunding platform? What does LendingClub do? What is crowdsourcing and is that the same thing as crowdfunding? They may seem alike, but there are big differences between these new platforms that you should know.

Related: What Does a Multibillion-Dollar Corporation Want With Crowdfunding?

Here are the three essential things every entrepreneur should know about crowdfunding.

1. It's not microfinancing. You've probably already heard of Kiva, which connects individuals with money to people in developing countries who could use a small loan to help their businesses. Loans can be as small as $25 and are repaid (albeit with no interest) to the individual who lent the money.

Kiva is a microfinance, social movement trying to connect small-business owners in developing countries (most are women) to capital they otherwise wouldn't be able to access. That sounds a lot like crowdfunding, right? Well, it's not.

Why is Kiva not crowdfunding? Because microfinance exists with a social improvement purpose: to lend money and provide opportunities for others. It's the concept of Nobel Peace Prize recipient Muhammad Yunus.

From his own experience growing up in Bangladesh, he realized many wanted to run a business and raise themselves out of poverty, but lacked the initial funding to get a venture started. The idea of microfinance to extend loans to emerging entrepreneurs who were too poor to qualify for traditional bank loans was a way Yunus saw to improve lives.

He tested his own idea by creating Grameen Bank, which does exactly that. Kiva, among others, followed and the microfinance movement began.

2. It's not crowdsourcing. Crowdsourcing and crowdfunding sound alike, but they're very different.

The idea behind crowdsourcing is to bring together people for the improvement of ideas or projects. It's the idea that the community, the whole, is better and can accomplish more than the individual.

Probably the clearest and best example of crowdsourcing is Wikipedia. You use it all the time, you may have even contributed to an entry, but it's all sourced and written by individuals who want to contribute to the community source.

With crowdsourcing, it's about sourcing and sharing in the benefits of knowledge, instead of funding.

3. Prizes, debt or equity? Crowdfunding is individuals collectively pooling money to fund projects or ideas. In many ways this "new" concept is quite old.

In fact, if you think about it, taxes are in essence the original crowdfunding. Sure, they're compulsory, but the idea is still the same: individuals contributing what they can into a pool of funds to then put toward the support of a common goal or project (think roads, health care, defense, etc). If you can wrap your head around taxes, then you'll get the idea behind crowdfunding.

CHAPTER 3

-WORD OF MOUTH MARKETING (WMM)-(Evangelism):

Word of Mouth Marketing (WMM)- has been the best and the most effective way of marketing since the beginning of time. There has been no integrated marketing, marketing mix or marketing strategy that can negate Word of Mouth marketing. We all do it and we sometimes don't even know. We tell our family, friends and associates even our enemies sometimes, about products and services we use, either it's good or bad, this gives the mileage and reach about the brand awareness. Everyone may not be able to start and run their own business. We may not all be business men and women, but its obvious we all need more money. Financial stability is of importance, because the older we get, the more our financial needs increase. Network marketing is simply making money through referrals while you pay less and get paid for using the product. Word of Mouth is the most efficient marketing tool for Network marketing. Direct Communication using different devices is very useful. It's just Gossip. Stop wasting time on profane discussions and conversation. Convert gossip to a money making venture like some celebrity magazine. Gossip and make money.

NETWORK MARKETING (NM)-

Network Marketing is the marketing solution for brands to the present Global Financial Crisis. Network marketing is the solution to Move you from Debt to Wealth, from financial crisis to financial stability, its your way out of the present Economic meltdown. All network marketing requires is to spread brands with the Word of Mouth and Earn income by making more money without stress, you don't have to quit your job or stop your normal day to day activities. You will simply be making residual income, that way you will open multiple streams of income for yourself.

Now, That's Money Working for you. Other benefits may come with Network Marketing like, half price vacation deals on hotels, flights, restaurants, rental cars, cruises, and more, a situation where you pay little or nothing, to gain more or get a very high discount on products and services you pay for on daily bases, most especially your bills and groceries. You earn More money or points for using products and services and by telling your family, friends, associates, class mates, school mates, colleagues and everyone you come in contact with even your enemies, about products and services of a brand or different brands . We all know that the Economy of every country runs on the Commercial Strength and Market Value of the Goods and Services they Produce which determines their Revenue. The Government, Organizations, Companies and Businesses in any jurisdiction need Network marketing if they must survive in the present marketplace. Within the next few years, Network Marketing will determine the new market leaders and brands that will stand out in the Market Place.

FRIENDSHIP POINTS:-

START UPS AND SMALL BUSINESSES -

Another smart Investment move, to Make Money work for you, is to invest in Start Ups or buy into StartUps. Small Businesses have always been the driver of the micro Economy. Its not as complex as Macro Economy, with a complex value chain. You can easily understand the operations of a Small Business and get involved. The Financial report is simple, and profit and loss account is easily accessible. You don't have to wait till the end of another Financial Year before you review the Financial Report.

A single young lady, took a smart decision and made a calculated risk five years ago to invest in a start-up small business, by saving some percentage of her income.

Today the startup company is five years old now, She is now making six figures Return on Investment and married with kids.

Invest in prospective businesses. You are buying into a Bright Future. A bright future, does not appear in the future. You have to Think and Work your way into a bright future, because your imagination is your real future. Invest in Businesses you Understand how it works and how you can make returns on your investment.

MICRO BUSINESSES (MB)-

You might not know how to start your own business or run the daily operations of a Business, but you sure need more money and want to get Rich and Stay Wealthy. One of the secrets is to convert what you love doing or what you are already doing into Cash. Advertise your skills for free by Posting on Your skills, Talents and Expertise on Social Media, You can also advertise on different websites that offer advertising services to people who need services of a different sort , known as online marketing. List your passion, skills and talent on advert websites, some her free and some, you pay just a token to get your advert published. You don't really need an office to run a micro business or hire anyone to run a micro business. This way you don't run any overhead cost by paying bills. With your laptop, Internet connection and a Mobile Phone, you can successfully run a micro business ,make extra income and open multiple streams of income for yourself. This is so easy for anyone. Its effective and efficient, because you are a Sole Proprietor and you are your own Boss. You can work from home in your bedroom or your living room. You call the shots and Make the final decision.

Like I mentioned before, that your Talent, Passion, Skills, Expertise, Knowledge, Purpose and Calling can be a perfect pointer to your Wealth. Your Gold Mine is not Far fetched, It is right by around you as Opportunity, or it is Right inside you as your Talent and Gift.

Open your mind, It's all about your mind-set, You can never rise above and beyond how You Think...As you think so you are. If you think rich, you will eventually get rich. The First Step to become Rich, is changing the way you think and renew your MIND. You have to start by Thinking Rich. You need to think like the rich. Change your thought process because the way you think attracts what comes into your life like people, situations, circumstances, finance, good fortunes, blessings and goodwill. If you think rich you will attract money and rich people in your life. You will talk like the rich and you will live like the rich.

It's not wishful thinking, it's not day dreaming, its not by talking about money, its more from your mind and heart and not your head. It's deliberate success consciousness, taking practical actions step by step. Your mind picture (Imagination) is the reflection of your real future. Your mind is the camera, and your memory is the mirror that reflects the pictures you store in your memory. You have the right to delete the wrong pictures and information, that sets you back and Leave the pictures and information that motivates you, keeps you happy and encourage you, to keep the positive flow of energy around you.

CHAPTER 4.

Let us talk about what Rich People Do- To Get Rich, You have to Do what Rich People Do. Never say what you don't mean and never make promises you can't keep.
This Rich book will teach you to become Money Smart, Street Smart, Work Smart and Book Smart and you will Know What Smart People Do. Make this book Your Wealth Navigator...

"The Rich People in the World are not the Smartest, the Smartest work for the Rich to make them richer", but the Smart work WITH the Rich.
Let me share with you the Attributes of the Rich. If you don't build your dream, you will help others build there's

They are Determined-

Determination is their driving force to surmount any obstacle that comes their way. Once they think of a solution and the way forward, they never doubt. They don't ask themselves or their team,"What If". They don't see impossibilities, they see only possibilities and they believe in themselves and they believe nothing is Impossible.

The best time to get rich is now. Now is the best time to get rich, tomorrow is not guaranteed. Follow me as I take you through my two decades of experience of working with the richest self made men and women of our time.

In the boardroom during an executive session amongst the executive directors of a multi billion dollar group of companies, existing for over a century. It was a critical moment since the company's inception, as some of the staffs are about to be laid off and some executives forced to resign. The company shares have drastically dropped to its all time low. Competitors had taken over the market as they presented customers with more valued added services and gave customers value for their money. The executives were clueless and had no where to turn to, they made consultations with the best agencies, and consultants, yet all their efforts fell through.

After several days of meetings and several hours of rigorous critical thinking, the final decision was about to be made, and letters were already typed, ready to be signed and sent to the affected staffs expected to be laid off and executives forced to resign. The meeting took a break for final recession and requested for coffee to be served. During coffee session, the executives were lamenting the failure of the company and groaning amongst themselves on how the so successful company is finally coming to an end, with no solution.

As coffee is being served round and some executives reluctantly sipping their coffee, while some couldn't even drink their cup of coffee at all. The attendant keenly listened to the conversation amongst the Executive Directors in the Boardroom, but carefully minding his own business. After serving everyone their cup of coffee before leaving the board room, the attendant thought to himself after a while and turned to talk to the MD/CEO of the company for a second, he told the personal assistance to the Company boss he will like to tell the boss a confidential information. In retort, the personal assistant said no, that all the executives were in the middle of a serious corporate discussion.

The coffee attendant in confidence, told the Boss Personal Assistant that it was very important and that if he doesn't talk to the company boss at once, the damage may be worse than what the company was experiencing at the time. The Personal Assistant insisted and said NO way one more time. While the Coffee attendant and the Boss Personal assistant were going back and forth on their discussion, the Boss called the personal assistant's attention and asked him what was going on, then the personal assistant told the Boss that the coffee attendant as refused to leave after serving them coffee and has requested to talk to him, then Boss in surprise asked the Coffee attendant to come around to ask his question.

As the coffee attendant walks through the midst of the executives all eyes glanced in awe and disappointment at his interruption. When the coffee attendant finally found his way to the front of the meeting where the boss was standing, the Boss asked swiftly, What is it? At this point all the executives glanced strictly and unacceptably to the coffee attendant and all attention was focused on the coffee attendant. As the coffee attendant stood before the company boss, he said' Sir, I have the Solution. Suddenly everyone turned to one another and mourmoured'. Some, mocked him in silence while others stood in disbelief. Looking straight into the Boss's eyes in self confidence and self belief. He told the company Boss Three words. "Increase the Diameter". What? The company Boss, retorted and thought about what the coffee attendant just said." Increase the Diameter. Then the Light Bulb came on, everyones mind was once again lighted-up and immediately the company boss called off the coffee session and requested the meeting should continue with immediate effect. As the session resumed the company boss requested that the coffee attendant stay behind for the remaining time of the meeting and was offered a seat with the executives. Every other person asides the company executives and the coffee attendant were excused from the meeting. The company boss immediately called for the presence of all the company's agencies and consultants, When everyone showed up.

The Company Boss in delight, welcomed everyone and with so much joy and gladness in his heart, he introduced the company's coffee attendant and informed the coffee attendant to address the company executives, the company agencies and consultants, by repeating out loud what he told him a couple of minutes ago. The Coffee attendant confidently stood before all the company's executives, the company agencies and consultants , dressed in his black and white uniform neatly worn, his hair nicely cut and shaved beards. He repeated the three words again "Increase the Diameter". Everyone was astonished at his display of ingenious idea and uncommon solution. Their perception about him, with the executives and all in the Board meeting began to change and they started seeing him as a genius and a great individual. He was promoted to the post of the Chief Operating Officer and he was told to demand his offer at any price. That was how his story changed from being an office coffee attendant to being an Executive Director in a Multi Billion Dollar International Corporation. One of the Worlds Best Selling Toothpaste Makers.

His gift made room for him, he saw the opportunity and he took positive advantage of it, he showed his concern for the success and growth of the company. He was self confidence and had self-believe, he was spontaneous and never hesitated, He never gave in when the Boss' Personal Assistant said No. He only thought of the solution and saw his goal. He never responded with a negative attitude, He never saw the executives as enemies, the never told the Boss he was wasting money on unnecessary ventures to find solutions. He was focused, precise, coinscice, straight to the point and direct. If we check through history of stories that have changed and revolutionized our World till date, It's been similar. Like the Story of King David, Joseph in the land of Egypt. Joseph moved from prison to palace, The story of Abraham, Daniel and so on till date. Never hide your gift and talent.

Don't ever be intimidated by your present situations, fears, issues and circumstances, Never give up on yourself.

The best results always come out of the worst situations. This is the Best time to Get Rich, as people lose their jobs daily and bills pile up. The Economic Meltdown and depression the world is facing presently, its only announcing new Financial Giants of our time. Ideas, Inspirations, Innovations, Creativity, Possibilities will be witnessed in this World like never before.

This revolutionized the company, and saved a lot of people from losing their jobs and others being forced to resign.
Yours may not be the Three Letter Word, yours may just be one WORD and that brings to mind the advent of the INTERNET in the 90's and Facebook in the New Millenium. Information and Communication has never been this better, easier and faster since creation. Technology has added so much value to our lives that the World is no more a global village, but a "Control Room" Information and Communication Technology has taken over our lives.

Growing up as a young man in a small town, a suburb of the city, he desired so much to be rich, he ventured into several business areas of interests but failed. Trade, service delivery, Transportation. He wondered why life is so unfair to him, he spends time thinking over what he is not doing right. He was hard working, he spends prudently, he never cut corners or involved himself with unethical business activities. Doing business seems not to be my thing he sobbed. Even though he knew he had very little level of formal education, he was very convinced that, you don't really have to be book smart to have a successful business. Finally he decided to work with his uncle who owns a transport business operating with just one commercial cab. His uncle has been in the transportation business for over ten years. He resumed work with no clue whatsoever of what his job description is and the responsibilities will be.

He his to assist his uncle with car wash, loading and offloading customers luggage into the trunk of the car and whenever business is slow, he will walk around the market place and inner streets to get customers for his uncle. He did this for a couple of years, while working with his uncle. He met lots of customers and made friends with some of them, he was always willing to assist and help. He was loved by everyone, because he always responds with a good attitude. We can Relate this story with Reproduction of a child from conception to birth and growth. Also making reference with seed time and harvest.He saved some of his income and earnings, to start his own transportation business and later advanced to the haulage business for top oil & gas firms. He became the third richest man in his country. He always credits his success secret to the mentorship by his uncle.

CHAPTER 5.

THE LADY STOREKEEPER.

She takes inventory and stocks of all the items and products supplied to their store location on a daily bases when she comes to work. This young lady works with one of the Largest stores in the United States of America. This particular day, a customer came around to buy a cosmetic product, in her store location. The customer searched and searched for this facial cosmetic product but never found it. After a futile search for over half an hour, She decided to ask this young lady about the possibility of the cosmetic product being available in stock. She walked up to the lady in disappointment to ask her, where the product can be found. Confidently the young store lady answered and said, yes we have the product in stock, kindly check isle 8 at the bottom. While their conversation was going on in search for the cosmetic item, other shoppers were minding their own business but faintly listening to their conversation.

The customer went back to continue searching, using the new instruction as directed by the young lady. A loyal customer, who always shops at this particular store location, who has been listening to their conversation while eavesdropping, walked up to the young store lady and gave her a wonderful idea.
He said, excuse me, " Yes, I noticed the other customer was right because, most of the time I also come here to shop, I sometimes have to search for a long time before I finally find, the item I want to purchase at this store location. I will like you to suggest to your management and the owners of this Store, that, Just as you have labeled the Isles from 1-10, Why don't you label the Numbered Isles in Alphabetical Order, In a simple illustration that he gave the young lady.

" Isle 1,A-D, Isle 2,A -D and recurring for each Isle from 1-10. That way, all you need to tell your customers in order to avoid , the needless long search for just an item, is, " Sir or Madam, kindly check Isle 4,D for what you are looking for. You will save time and energy for the customer and yourself and the Store in general will look more professional. This customer advised the young store lady and she took the advice. At the stores next staff meeting, this young store lady pitched this sales strategy to the Supervisor and the Management. Guess what, She was promoted to the position of the Manager and instantly became the boss to her colleagues. Her income tripled and she started training other junior staffs. This same Idea has been replicated in all their store Outlets throughout the United States of America, and this store stands as one of the most outstanding stores in the United States, known for their customer Satisfaction.

CINEMA RAVE-

The Story of Cinema, Rave and The Loyalty Reward Money Card for Students on Books, Music and Dining, Vacations and Entertainment, Mobile Radio. Dial to Listen, Listen to vote- As a college student, something was missing in the extra-curriculum activity of the university.

He gained admission into one of the best Ivy League Schools in his Country on Merit to Study Business Management. While in school, he discovered that there is something missing in the students extra-curricullum activities. Young people are full of life, and they always want to find every slightest opportunity to express themselves. There is so much energy around and everyone is full of life, but they have little means of expressing themselves. They are very studious and desire to be successful in their careers and in life. Parents, Guardian and Visitors could tell, how much they feel the energy of the students anytime they come visiting their wards on campus.

This student thought to himself one day, that what can he do to add value to the extra-curriculum activities of the students.

After a while an idea popped up in his mind called "Cinema Rave". He said, the Cinema Movie location is a bit far from the school and students will hardly want to take the long ride to the cinemas and pay to watch movies and also buy popcorn and drink while watching an interesting movie. Students in the school only do this on holidays and a special day like Valentine's day. He was trying to bring fun back to school and create a tranquil atmosphere amongst students. Since the school premises were not built to accommodate a Movie, Cinema, and he can't create one on the school campus. He said " He can take the Students to the Cinemas and Bring them back to School after the movies. After, thinking through his idea thoroughly, he decided to offer the closest Cinema location a deal, where they will pick a particular day of the week say mid-week, when it's not prime time for the movie halls, To bring interested students to the cinemas to watch their choice movie in the Box Office and they can also get a popcorn and drink to go with it and get a VIP admission into the A-list Lounge for an after party.

The Cinema Facility Owner was delighted about this light bulb idea and he gladly welcomed it. The student and his team were able to negotiate a nice deal with the Cinema Owner to get a half price of the Normal cost. Now, transporting the students from the school to the Cinemas and back was another challenge. So they thought to themselves, how to surmount this challenge. After a while, they decided to hire executive luxury buses from a reputable transportation company. They were able to negotiate a good deal and the Transport company agreed. In return for an advert on publicity and awareness material, the transportation company offered the first trip free for all the students. The students were delighted about this and they Cinema Rave started in July 2009.

They were able to charge each student, same price they would have paid just to watch only the movies without transportation, popcorn and drink, the same price for all inclusive to get a Movie Ticket with, Transportation, Popcorn and Drink and Lounge at an after Party . They made a profit doing this and extended the same fellowship to Neighboring schools, who gladly hop-on to the moving train, soon enough they gained mighty followers. This idea afforded the innovative students the opportunity to sponsor themselves with tuition fee and accommodation, during their remaining years in College.

CHAPTER 6.

MOBILE MONEY PAYMENT SOLUTION-(Banking the Unbanked).

Cash exchange and moving cash, became a huge challenge as accountability could not be ascertained. Cash Exchange can be challenging when huge sum of money is involved. Collating, Counting and Calculating money can be challenging if it's done by people with their bare hands. Putting the collected monies together and remitting it to the accountant can be challenging also. This became a challenge that has to be tackled and solved. This became so worrisome due to the large amount of money coming in on weekly bases. The young students thought to themselves on how they can administer a lasting solution to their Cash-flow. This spurs them to reason on the closest companion of every student, which is their mobile phones. They discover that every student spends more time on their mobile phone than they do after class, even when they are with their friends, they still tweet, post messages on Facebook and share pictures on Instagram. Texting has become a culture in and out of classrooms, reducing the talk time and discussions among each other.

To make payment easier for the weekly Cinema Rave activity which as become a norm amongst all the students and spreading like wild fire to all other colleges and high schools the Creators of Cinema Rave decided to introduce what is called mobile payment to the students. A situation where they can pay for the Weekly Event via their mobile phones, in different categories, you can pay for a week, a month, a semester or a season Cinema Rave Ticket. What the mobile payment does is, that the students created a payment app, where the students can download for free on their mobile phones and different mobile devices and send payment for their ticket via the app.

They can choose different payment options and instantly have the Cinema Rave ticket delivered to their phone by email with the corresponding bar code. The bar code carries the details of individual ticket buyer or group purchase.

This way the Cinema Rave Creators were able to eliminate the Cash Challenge of Collecting, Collating, Counting and Remitting the large amount of Cash. This mobile payment option soon developed into what they call Mobile Money, a situation where students were able to transfer money via their mobile phones.

They introduced the Mobile Money to their parents, families and friends, who use this same mobile payment solution to Transfer Money to them. Shortly after the introduction of Mobile Money as a payment solution for Cinema Rave and other utilities. They soon took it a step further by adding more value after a year to introduce a Loyalty Card for students. The loyalty card came in the form of ATM Credit/Debit Card where Students can earn pointss for using the ATM card at different Point of Sales Terminal (POS) and earn point that can be converted to cash and these points can be used to purchase in different Select Outlets and Stores.

They were able to Partner with major Banks and Financial institutions and they soon had all the major sales outlets join from Books and Libraries, to Clothing and Fashion, to Shoes, Groceries, Make-ups, Entertainment and Events, Sporting Tickets, Movie Tickets, Vacation Rental, Flights, Tourist Attractions, Hotels & Hostels, Cinemas, Movies, Transportation, Dining and Restaurants. The Team of Young Creators were able to build a Brand from an Idea to an International Franchise. Soon the "Cinema Rave" concept developed from an idea to a Merchandise.

DIAL TO LISTEN & LISTEN TO VOTE- (D2L & L2V) FOR SYNDICATED T.V SHOWS.

Syndicated Talent Show became a Toast of TV audience at the time, and the Interest grew among viewers by the season. But there was a challenge. Watching each episode regularly at the set time for the show. Brands were eager to sponsor and advertise with the different Reality TV talent shows, and the Franchise owners, were working day and night to make the shows more interesting and engage the audience interest through more interactive medium. Filling the Gap and bridging the missing link became the challenge to be tackled. The Viewing Audience is spreading like wildfire, but the level of interaction and audience engagement was declining compared to the viewing. The prime time show became a routine for all T.V watchers.

At that time, the Brand company and ad agency were about rolling out a new campaign and Brand Activation. They had informed all the copywriters and storytellers to work on the best pitch for the Campaign and Activation for the best possible publicity ATL (Above The Line) and BTL (Below The Line) awareness campaign.

After long hours of the mastermind alliance in the war room meeting, he stepped back into his office to relate the outcome of the meeting with his subordinates being the HOD (Head of Department). While he was briefing his department, tension grew, among them and the responsibility to deliver the desired result falls on all of them. They were all in the quiet mode and sober mood as they have no clue where to turn to for the best possible result. During the meeting, one of the department members was busy checking his phone, for messages on Social Media and His text messages. His excited girlfriend was, busy narrating the performances she saw the previous night, and she was busy narrating the story to her boyfriend, who was meant to be busy focus of the meeting, while his phone is meant to be turned off during the time of the meeting.

In the course of the meeting he HOD noticed the distraction, and yelled at him. "Hey You" Adam, what are you doing? He asked expressing his anger and disappointment. Adam looked up in a split second and all eyes were on him. He dropped his phone to the side in response and was speechless and dumbfounded, with no words to say. He looked ashamed , as the Boss poured out his dissatisfaction and disappointment in him. " See me after the meeting he told the boy,.

The meeting was over and everyone went back to their duty posts to get back to work. The HOD, furiously walked back to his office, looking so provoked, he slammed the glass door behind him. The boy came to the HOD's office and knocked the glass door gently. " Come in, the HOD Screamed at him. Stepping into the HOD's office with so much fear and shame, he looked down. The HOD stood by his table, staring at the boy like he was going to react. The boy pleaded, and asked for a last warning, apologetic, he told the HOD he will never disrespect the department during any meeting ever again he promised. The Boss said, in response to the boy's apologies, that "If it ever happens again, He will have him suspended indefinitely. " Yes Sir, the boy altered in a sigh of relief. After a short minute of silence, the HOD asked the boy, "So what solution can you proffer to the Challenge we have on the ground. The Boy said, Sir, " I was just thinking if this Idea can help the client, solve this challenge. " I was thinking, If we Introduce Dial-To-Listen to engaging the viewing audience, and make the Talent Show more Interactive. A situation where Viewers can dial a short code number to Listen to their favorite contestant. This will make the show more interactive and audience friendly.

CHAPTER 7.

By listening to their Mobile Phones, Viewers can take control of their time and listen to their mobile phone at anytime. That way, they won't miss any part of the show. They can also Listen-To-Vote for their favorite Audience Real Time, after they Dial-To-Listen. In the same they Dial-To-Listen, They can Watch the show on their Mobile phone Real Time, via online streaming and they can also Vote Online. Instantly, the HOD made a call to the Technical Department to Share the Possibility and the Feasibility of the idea, The Technical department gave a Nod, to the idea and said yes, it was possible, that all they need to do, is to upload data on servers at their Work Station and Remotely Control the Dual way Communication Traffic, in order to avoid, Congestion and Disruption of Telecommunication. The News soon reached to the Clients and the Title Sponsors and they were all delighted for the Break Through.
This idea won the boy a tongue wagging six figure contract with the Brands and Got married to his Girlfriend.

Dial To Listen to mobile radio, is developed for mobile phone users to listen to radio on their mobile phones and listen to their favorite music without internet connection, for a token of 50 cents per minute, mobile phone users can dial simple, short code numbers to listen to Mobile Radio, for their favorite radio shows, music and their favorite on air radio personalities. The pilot for the idea was tested successfully, during the pilot and testing mode, and as been accredited as the future and Revolution of Radio, better than satellite and Internet radios. With the advent of Mobile Radio, Listeners can filter what they listen to online and the Media. Listeners have the power to control, their own content, they listen to. No internet or Download is required for mobile radio. All it requires is a code number or a direct link to the music database and listeners playlist.

Cinema Rave "Mobile Movie On Demand" - Mobile Movies Distribution.

Mobile Movies On Demand (MMD) was developed by the Founders and Creators of Cinema Rave, to afford people that can't make it to the cinemas to watch the latest release movies in the box office. A mobile Movie App was developed for this purpose, and what movie lovers need to do is to download the movie app on their phones, and subscribe to New Movies in the box office, for as long as they desire. starting from seven days, to one month and then three months, six months and a year. The Mobile Movie App can be downloaded on mobile phones and any mobile device and the latest movies can be watched on the day of release as convenient it is for people to watch at the cinemas. Through their subscription movie lovers will pay for the movies to be watched on their mobile devices as individuals or as a group on their tablets.

MOBILE MARKETING-

You can provide and make food supplies available via Mobile Food Trucks, a friend suggested to a major restaurant food chain . That way you will eliminate the bottleneck of having to make several deliveries every day. All you need do is to drive the Food Truck around to high areas and places of high footfall. Places where lots of people gather on daily bases. That way you will increase sales and maximize profits by adding more value to your product line. You also have the opportunity of publicity and awareness through Mobile Advertising to a Large Crowd with the Branded Mobile Food Truck.

Business Connections, Corporate Appointments and Meetings-

The Hotel Lobby, was well equipped with modern interior facilities glowing and dazzling with different array of designs, from crystal chandeliers, to expensive furniture, glass, frames, tiles and precious detailed finishes. The Restaurant filled with top of the class dining wares at a distance. The Bar and Lounge stocked up with top shelf drinks, waiting for customers to start patronage within a couple of hours. Quietly sitting by the pool side of the hotel, glancing through a copy of the Time Magazine, relaxing in the cool of the day, sipping a glass of champagne. He decided to step into the lobby to stretch his legs for a few minutes being that he his been relaxing at the hotel pool side for like two hours. Stepping into the lobby after a few seconds, he looked up, and behold a smart looking professional corporate lady, walked in, neatly dressed in her skirt and blouse, wearing a black 4 inch high hill designer shoes. She carried a handbag to match, paying attention to details. Her hair well packed, her nails well polished, wearing a feminine well scented perfume moderately. She walked through the hallway and then through the lobby, all eyes glancing at her charismatic looks and excellent persona.

She went straight to the coffee bar, pulled a comfy chair out and sat elegantly like a well trained professional. She turned to her bag, reached for her iPad and flipped it opened. Reading through a presentation, while waiting for her meeting appointment. Within five minutes of sitting down, He walked up to her with a smile on his face, he broke the long silence and said, hi, and introduced himself, politely the lady responded and introduced herself in return. The man asked, you must be here for a high net worth meeting I guess. She said, sure, you must be smart to recognize that. He smiled and said, yes, it's written all over you. You look like you are here for a serious business meeting. Well, what do you do he asked.

She said I am a Financial Advisor, and I work with an International Financial Institution on Investment Banking and Wealth Management. That's awesome he said.

To satisfy his curiosity and quest to meet the beautiful lady he asked, so what brought you here? In response she said " I am here on an Appointment to meet with a client for a very important high net worth meeting. The client will be here any moment from now and the meeting will commence. Here is my Business Card. Call me. Then, she asked, what do you do? In response he said " I am a Business Consultant with special competence to Investment in the Real Sector. Good, she said in amazement. She probed further by asking, What is your largest portfolio and Account, Non at the moment, but I hope to partner on a huge project soon. Then he added that he can handle projects in Major Real Sectors and different Businesses interests. Well, "What time will you be less busy tomorrow, she asked him. He said evening time. "Call me to make an Appointment. she said, to end their conversation.
They met the next day as agreed, for their business meeting appointment where they discussed different areas of business interests at length. After a couple of minutes of in depth business discussion and insightful business analysis. The man got hired as a Financial advisor and Investment Consultant for the International Financial Institution.

CHAPTER 8.

RESOURCE MANAGEMENT-

Human existence is programmed in the time space. Time is the most essential and the most valuable resource of mankind, and it's the only Resource has given to everyone in the same measure. Regardless of age, status, location, gender, color and race. We all have equal amounts of time every day. We may not all come from rich parents or rich families, but we all have 24 hours a day to achieve whatever we desire and assigned to do. The difference between the Rich and the Poor is the Effective Management of their time. There are a lot of people from rich families and rich parent, that are properly poor, so it doesn't matter to your family background or status. You can spend money anyhow you want, You can waste money on anything you wish, but you can never waste time anyhow. Time is Money, we all agree. We all get paid in accordance and commensurate, based on our productivity per time or per hour. People pay for your skill based on time. If you value time, you value money. I wrote in the review of this book that Wealth Creation and Riches, is More about Adding Value than, Having Money. Time is Money, Manage your time wisely never Waste Time, Its the Greatest Resource of Mankind, It's Never Too Late, You can Start Afresh or Change Your game plan.

MONEY MANAGEMENT-

BUDGETING & COST CUT.

There is no reason why you should live above your means for any reason. You've got no one to impress. You can get rich with peace of mind, if you learn to live within and below your means. Spend Smart.

1 Pitcher Draft Beer, and 4 shots of Tequila please, open tab, Nick called the bartender's attention to his table. With arrogance he spoke out loud to his friends, I am a huge spender, Nick boastfully tells all his friends. I don't save money, I spend money. I am good at spending, and I don't care because I know, I will always live to make money. I spend it as I make it. These were the words he boastfully uttered to his friends at the bar, sipping his glass of beer, while his friends and associates sit and stare at him. You only live once, He continued, what if you die tomorrow, it's whatever you spend your money on, that will reverberate and echo on with you, in your grave, when you are dead. He further said, hey, guys you know what," No matter how much money you have left in your bank account, when you die, it's your family and friends that knew nothing about how you made your money, that will fight their way to spend it after you die. I live to enjoy my life a day at a time. I don't care about tomorrow. I spend it as I make it. That is my life. During his proud talk, a commercial flashed on the T.V Set, it was an advert interval during a football game. Then he paused to view the message with his friends. The advert was about different houses on foreclosure up for the cheapest sales, in his county.

The houses for sale are selling for as low as $240. Then the phone number to call in for interested buyers ended the commercial. Yes, there are lots of houses in this community up for foreclosure, for such a low price, his friend Jason, said. I hope I can grab this opportunity while it last. Jason further asked Nick, Hey, Nick, Is it possible, if you can loan me like 240 bucks. Nick Said, in affirmation, absolutely, when do you need it. Jason said, as soon as possible. Nick replied, well I don't have up to $240 right now in my Bank account, but I hope to get my paycheck in the next couple of days. Yes, I will loan you, but when do you hope to pay me back. Jason Told him, once I am able to get myself on my feet with my new job, I will definitely pay you back. Meanwhile, when the commercial was advertised, Jason took down the advertised phone number for interested buyer on his phone, with the intention to call for more information.

Few days later, Jason got the loan from Nick for $240, on friendship Terms and Trust.

Jason, called the company offering the foreclosure houses for sale, and he was called for a meeting, which he attended to sign the necessary papers for the Transfer of ownership of his name, like the deed, C of O and Property Tax papers. He got the papers, and went back home as a proud home owner.

Meeting with his friends, later that evening at the bar, he announced his new property acquisition. His friends congratulated him in awe, as they never believed Jason, the jobless guy, could be a home owner, just by making a smart decision. Nick, interrupted and said, let's drink to celebrate Jason's New achievement, I sponsored him and I am proud. Hey Bartender, 2 pitcher draft beer and 4 Tequila shots for me and my friends. All drinks on me. They all drank and were merry.

While in the celebration mood. Jason was busy thinking and trying to figure out what to do with his new property. Everyone joyfully returned home, hoping to meet the next day after work. Weeks later, Jason's phone rang, and it was an interested buyer. A millionaire, who invests in real estate. told his attorney and agents, to get properties, in Jason's county for the purpose of building a five star hotel. The Millionaire was ready to pay his way to get the property.

Jason's property became a perfect toast to the project. Jason, was contacted and he was informed about the new development. Jason agreed to the terms of the purchase, and a lease contract was signed for $940,000 for 20 years. Jason became rich. He ever since then made millions of dollars in Real Estate Investment. He paid back his friend Nick the loan repayment of $240 with an appreciation gift of $60 making $300. 20 years later Jason's net worth was over $1.5 Billion. Unfortunately Nick died broke, he was bankrupt.

We can relate Jason's experience, with that of a Tech Guru, who registered a domain name, then in the late 90's/New millennium. He was able to register a common domain name in the .com for free then. Within 5 years. He sold his domain, through a website sales bid for over $9,000,000. ($9 million).

Money Management, is all about your prudence with money. Your life right now and your financial status, is a result of how prudent you are, spending money and making money. You are either saving, investing or spending money.

CHAPTER 9.

FRIENDSHIP POINTS-

Retailers, will have to draw up new sales strategies and market tactics for the growing trend of product and Market savvy consumers in this 21st century. Using friendship points to sell, their goods. Friendship points, is a sales strategy, just like Network marketing. Let me show you How that work. I am walking through a mega shopping mall in the city, and a young lady, walked up to me to market and sell their cosmetics range of products to me, she did this by taking a quick shot survey, by asking some questions. I answered all her questions, then she said why, don't you come into our store, to check the products for testing, you can then decide to buy any of the products you may be interested in.
Unfortunately, I had to make a quick transaction at the bank, and I was running late, if i don't get to the bank in 10 minutes, the banks will be closed. I was left with 2 decisions. Either to please the young lady, by following her to the store or stick to my plans to go to the bank to make my transaction, in order to complete my to-do-list for the day. I am sorry, I got to go, I told the young lady, in empathy.

The young lady, did a good job to market and sell the product. She promoted the product, in a way that caught my attention, but unfortunately, time did not permit her to close the deal.Then I thought to myself, only if retailers can develop the Friendship points sales strategy to sell, that way, they can sell more to a lot of people, and they can build a customer base for family and friends. All Friendship Points entail is, referring family and friends, to buy a particular product or good for its peculiarity, and you the referral can earn friendship points, the more people you refer the more your points. These points can be used to purchase products and goods, at the store, depending on the number of points, you have been able to accumulate over the time through your referral.

Money Management, Tax & Accounting.

The Book smart don't break the rules. They bend the rules in their favor. Never you break the rules, because you can end up in jail, dead or get fired. Don't be a party to the "Don't get Caught" syndrome. Some people believe it's cool to break the rules, but don't be caught. NO. The smart don't break the rules rather they bend the rules in their favor. The Reason a lot of people evade tax is simply because they are not wise. The Rich don't Evade Tax, They may be late in paying their Taxes, but they never evade taxes, because they know the consequences in the long run. Paying Taxes is a way of giving back to the society that gave you the opportunity to become rich and get wealthy. The government in turn uses the taxes to Build schools, Health Facilities, Good Means of Transportation, Service the Government, Protect and Defend the Country, lives and Properties and for Social Amenities and Facilities.

The Money Smart declares their tax after residual profit, called profit after tax. The reason you have to be rich, is to be smart with your income and know how to Manage your Cash Flow, Your Cost, Your Income or Revenue, your Spending or Expenditure. Your Regular Budget, Money Management. Account Statement, Balance Sheet, Credit and Debit and Profit and Loss Account.

CHAPTER 10

THE STOCK MARKET -

Stock Exchange- Buy Low & Sell High (BL & SH) Is the Profit Rule.

Investing in shares is One of the most prudent investment of all time, investing in Shares or Stocks of a company is very wise. Buying Shares is more advisable than saving up for nothing. Never you tie your money down in your bank account. Invest it, that way, you have planted seeds on good soil, to anticipate an harvest in season in form of profit and wealth. If you are not really into Stocks or buying shares. I will advise you set some money aside to buy some shares for Your kids. Start setting Financial Goals for your Future. A Generation that does not invest in the future of the kids have no future. As a shareholder of any company, you have become a co-owner of that company, No matter their years of existence and their profit margin annually. Even if you cannot create a trust fund for your kids education from elementary to college. You can buy into company shares for them to be Financially Independent as they grow. Investing in stocks is a wise choice and I will advise you on how to go about it.

Buy shares when the prices are low. Financial Intelligence is of paramount importance if you must be Rich and Wealthy. Your knowledge about the stock market must be up to date if you want to be a successful investor in stocks. Your shares will appreciate as the price increase and you can sell when prices are all time high. Meaning you buy Shares, when the prices are at all time low and you sell when the prices are at All time High. You will make money this way and you can become a big player in the stock market. You will need to seek the advice of experts in the Stock Market like Stock Brokers if you want to be good success in the Stock Market.

You can buy shares in Beverage Companies, Financial Institutions, Oil and Gas, Real Estate, I.T, Communications, Food and Agriculture. Let me give you a wise counsel. Buy Shares in companies that have stood the test of time, and Companies that People cannot do without using the products on a daily bases. Seek the advice of Stock Brokers, Money Managers or Investment Advisors help you decide on the best options available.

At 16, he bought his first set of shares by investing in stocks of one of the most reputable Beverage and Brewing companies in the World at a National Stock Market with the help of the local Stock Brokers. The share value at that time was $1 per share. He was able to put together his pocket money in his savings and the money he made from selling books by his mentors. He sold Inspiring books he read to his friends at half price. After a while of self discipline and staying focused he was able to gather $100 to purchase Shares of the Multinational Company. Then the shares cost $1 per share. He purchased $100 value which makes it 100 shares. He received his Share Certificate later as a proof of becoming a shareholder in that company. Months later the Shares of the company Rose from $1 per share to $5.50 per share, that brings the value of his shares to $750, from $100. He sought the advice of his Stock Brokers and decided to sell 50% of his Shares value. He then made a profit of $375.

During the period of this Transaction, an International Financial Institution just acquired a Bank and Merged with two other Major Banks to form a Global Finance House. They have Issued an Initial Public Offer (IPO) and offer their stocks to be sold in the Stock Market.
The 16 year old boy now 19, bought into the Shares of the International Bank with his proceeds from the Transaction of his shares from the first company.
Ten years down the line, He sits as an Executive Director in Major International and National Companies, in different major sectors of the

Economy and he presides over his own company.
That can also be your story. It's not too late to start.

What is important is for you to start, don't procrastinate, do it now. Start Now. Tomorrow might be too late. Like I said in the beginning that Money is not a permanent friend. Money is a Temporary Visitor and It's what you do with Money, that makes Money to either stay with you forever to make you rich and Wealthy, or Fly away from you, to make you broke and poor.

The Opportunity is right there staring at you before your very eyes, glancing and waving to you, Recognize it, Discover it and Convert it into Real Value, then you can become Rich and Wealthy. You can not keep waking up every day of your life and allow opportunities to pass you by on daily bases. It's like Winking to a beautiful girl in the dark. This terminology is also used in Marketing. They say, " Having a good product without Marketing or Advertising it, is like Winking to a Beautiful girl in the Dark". No matter how good or great a product is, without Marketing it, it's going to be short lived or never get to the consumers. The reach will be limited. Like I mentioned in the beginning that the Marketplace is not about who is right or wrong, but who is successful. Consumer Marketing is very important in the Value Chain and Production Process of any Corporation.

CHAPTER 11.

THE MONEY MARKET-

Foreign Exchange (ForEx)-

Trading Forex can be another area of investment to explore. One of the Major Trade secrets of the Banks, Financial Institutions and the Rich, is Foreign Exchange. They Trade with money in the Bank. Foreign Exchange is simply buying and selling of currencies in respect to Demand and Supply. The same way you go shopping at the grocery or supermarket for goods and products. That's how the Rich Trade Forex. They shop for Valuable currencies to Trade with. They compare the value of the currencies to the Dollar Rate as of that day and time, and they Buy or Sell the Currency. They Buy when the prices are Low and Sell when the Prices are High.

You must have been thinking to yourself, that why are the Rich getting Richer and the Poor Getting Poorer. The simple Reason is that, the Rich will never leave their Money lying In any Bank Account, just because, they know money will not produce any result if it's not well invested. You get back what You put in. It's Garbage In-Garbage Out. The Rich Will always Trade their Money Either as Investment or as ForEx. They check the Exchange Rate of different currencies on a daily bases as Compared with the $USD. They seek the advice of their Money Mangers or Investment Banker before taking their decision. Then with the Help and Assistance of their Advisors, they then Go ahead to Trade or Instruct their Investment Banker to Trade certain amount of Money, for the best prices in the Money Market.Demand and Supply, Cost and Pricing, Production and Inflation, are always the effect of different factors and are affected by different factors.

The burden falls on the consumers and determines Consumer Behavior.

Buy when the currency exchange rates are Low and Sell when the currency exchange rates are High compared to the $USD.

His phone rang one morning, and "Hello" he answered, How are you? Good morning, the conversation continued between an Investment Banker and his client. I am fine Sir, Good morning to you Sir. "Sir, I just checked right now, and I discovered that the Exchange rate is 1.99 to $1.00. Really the client responds. Yes Sir, the Investment Banker said. The client, double checked and tune into the Business News of the day, and discovered that the information from his Investment Banker was accurate. He further asked the Investment Banker what to do, the Investment banker Advised they sell. Then Sell $1000 worth. The investment banker followed the client's instruction and he made profit huge profit of 99%. The same currency sold for .99 to $1.00 the last time they checked to Trade in the Money Market ForEx.

Every Cent Counts- When it comes to Investment, every cent counts. You will amazed to know that the Rich and Wealthy, make their Millions and Billions in Business from every little cents and pennies and not on the Huge Millions and Billions they Dream of or expecting from a Big Transaction Business Deal. Most time, their profit margin is usually between 1 cent to $10. They know every cent counts, and that is why they don't joke with figures. They gather as many facts as possible from Resources available to them and Seek the Advice of experts, like Financial Advisors, Investment Bankers, Money Managers, Business Consultants and Brokers to guide them through their decision making process. They concentrate on volume and mass quantity.

I know a certain Rich man, who is always having his Advisors around all the time, to help him make the best business decision. He surrounds himself with wise counsel.

He his a team player and a wise man indeed. He trades, by Investing in consumer goods, He did so well that, he won a contract to Import more of the consumer goods and supply all the distributors and Wholesalers, He soon became a Major Supplier to the Distribution Chain. Not long enough, he became a $ Billionaire. Guess what? his profit margin was only 42 cents on each item. If he supplied 10 million Units of that consumer item, guess how much profit that will sum up. What if he supplied 100 million Units or Better 1 Billion Units. In the multitude of Counsel indeed there is safety. Don't be too Arrogant to ask questions. The easiest and fastest way to get answers is when you ask. We all know better these days because we always ask Google. You should always seek advice from experts, professionals and people that know more than you, in any endeavor. It does no harm to anyone, It does a lot of good to you, because If you know better, you will do better. Ask and you shall be given, Seek and You shall find, Knock and the Door shall be opened. This Law and Principles can never fail, it has never failed and it will never fail. Droplets of Water make a mighty Ocean. Multiple Trees, makes a mighty Forest. Team Work, Works. If you walk, talk and work with the wise, you will be wise. If you walk, talk and work with fools, you will be foolish. Who are your friends and Associates? Show me your friend and I will tell you who you are.

CHAPTER 12.

FIXED DEPOSIT (FD)-

"Business is not My Thing" , Some Admit . If you have no flair or passion for doing business, You can still make money work for you, and make profit, from your money if you decide not to invest in any form Business. You can have your money fixed by your bank in a fixed deposit. Some people say " Business is not their Style. They prefer to work 9-5 , Live pay check to pay check, Pay their bills on time, Maintain a very good Credit Score, Save up enough in case of emergency and Live on Pension whenever they RETIRE. They always want to live by their means, Disturb nobody and want no worries from no one. This is common amongst Government Workers, Civil Servants, and Lots of Employees. But the Money Smart Employees, will not leave their Money Dormant in any Bank Account. You can deposit your Money in a fixed Account called fixed deposit, you may not have to re-open another account for this. Depending on the Tenure or Maturity Date Plan, varying from 7 days, 15 days, 45 days, 90 days, 1 year or 10 years, depending on your preference, as advised by your Bank or Financial Institution.

You can Roll Your Money Over after the tenure to elongate the duration and re-invest. You will make profit, according to the interest rate usually between 4% to 11% and how long you decide to keep your money in the fixed account. The profit depends on the interest rate declared by your Holding Bank or Financial Institution. Ask Your Account Manager how it works and The best practice you need to Make the most out of the fixed deposit. You can fix any amount as advised by your Financial Institution and Start with what you have. You can save up, for a fixed deposit, once the amount is right for you. Be convinced beyond every reasonable doubt before you proceed. Understand how it works and if you are satisfied with the proceeds and the Returns on Investment.

A fixed deposit is a financial instrument provided by banks which provides investors with a higher rate of interest than a regular savings account until the given maturity date. It is also known as a term deposit, time deposit or a bond. They are considered to be very safe investments. The defining criteria for a fixed deposit is that the money cannot be withdrawn from the Fixed Account before maturity. Some banks may offer additional services to Fixed Account holders such as loans against Fixed Deposit certificates at competitive interest rates. These investments are safer. They also offer income tax and wealth tax benefits.

REAL ESTATE & PROPERTY INVESTMENT (REI).

Land Properties still remain, the most Potent Source of Wealth, anywhere in the World, and one of the Most Valuable Assets anyone can possess, because it hardly depreciates in Value, depending on Location, the Soil type and Potential Resources. Land Lords, Home Owners and Real Estate Agents. Hotels, Apartments, Accommodation, Houses, Homes and Buildings either for office Buildings or Commercial purposes, Can never go out of fashion and can never be out dates Investment.

THE GOLD MARKET (GM) GOLD COINS & GOLD BARS Bullion Trading. (BL.SH) The Buy Low and Sell High profit Rule is also applicable.

Your Billions can start with Trading Bullion. Precious Metals and Precious Stones, Are as valuable as cash. Gold, Silver, Platinum and Diamonds can be accepted for their cash value. You can save Gold, Silver,

Platinum and Diamond same way you bank your money. The Value on precious metals and precious stones always appreciates in a stable market without inflation. Gold, along with silver, has long been known as the primary means of real money.

For thousands of years, gold has been used in trade. It is real, scarce, cannot be artificially reproduced, and has inherent value. Gold has stood the test of time more than any other form of currency. You won't find any other paper money or notes that was around hundreds of years ago, but you will see that gold is just as in demand now as it was then.

Gold coins are perhaps the most recognizable staple in the gold and silver bullion industry. Coins offer value in their bullion content and scarcity alike. While gold bars and bullion can be produced in many different ways and in almost any quantity, gold coin will always have a relative scarcity. Once a set year of production for a gold coin is complete, there will not be another edition of that coin produced. Beyond this, coins also offer the peace of mind that comes along with knowing your gold was minted by a well known and respected mint, like the US Mint or the Royal Canadian Mint.

Gold coins do cost more than gold bars in most cases, but much, if not all of this cost is recovered in their typical sell value. If you prefer to own bullion that is produced by the most trusted mints in the entire world, gold coins are an optimal choice. Gold coins also serve as legal tender in almost every nation in which they are produced, whereas gold bars do not. Whether you are interested in a fractional gold coins or several ounces at a time, gold coins will help to accomplish your goals in gold bullion.

To be be a successful player in the Gold Market and Precious Metal Industry, you have to update your knowledge about the market price on a daily bases. Just like the Stock Market and ForEx. You will need to work with experts and advisors, who will guide you and help you make a sound decision.

Today, there are a number of convenient ways to buy gold coins and other precious metals . Depending on your particular situation, investment objectives and bullion trading needs, you may decide to buy gold coins or. Invest in gold, silver, platinum or palladium outright in an all-cash purchase and have your purchase delivered to you. Or, you can have your purchase stored for you at one of several secure and independent banks and depositories. When you buy coins or bullion, you retain ownership of, and title to, the precious metals, and your precious metals are insured by the bank or storage facility.

You can explore and seek investment opportunities in Information and Communications Technology (ICT or I.T), Telecoms, Crude Oil & Gas, Agriculture & Farming, Transportation & Haulage, Education & Skill Acquisition, Distribution & Wholesale, Retail, Delivery & Sales Rep, Import & Export.

CHAPTER 13.

RESOURCE CONTROL (RC)-

Corporate Governance, Best Practices, Business Ethics, Standards and Bench Marks (Excellence and Quality).

Accountability and Responsibility are the soul of Resource Control. Responsibility keeps you in the perfect position for Resource Control. A Billionaire once said, that the two most difficult things to manage and control in the World is People and Money. Managing people is a very difficult task. If you can influence people, you will have other things under your control easily. Managing People is not easy at all. But if you develop the right skills to manage people, you will lead effectively, you will live rich and stay rich. You will be efficient in responsibility.

You will be able to manage people and their talent and you will Prudently manage resources. Resource Control has remained the major challenge of any individual leader, a family breadwinner, Corporate Executives and any government. The reason any Organization, Corporation, or any Nation can be considered as being corrupt is simply because of flaws in their Resource Control and Resource Management. From the little dimes to the multi-billion. every cent and penny count. Accountability is very crucial to Resource Control. If you are responsible, you will definitely be accountable , and if you are accountable, you will be responsible. A lot of individuals, families, corporations, organizations, institutions and Nations have failed simply because of Resource Control. Managing Scarce resources for maximum results, is a challenge, but once you are able to resolve and find a solution to resource control, you will be at the top of your game.

If you can not control Money, Money will control you, people have failed simply because they allowed money to control them. It does not matter if you have no money, before money can get hold of you, to control you. If you love money, it will control you, because all your decisions will be clouded by your love for money. You will not really know what to do to assist and help people, in terms of goodwill and charity, all your decisions will be financially motivated rather than being value motivated. The Richest and the Wealthiest are value driven and value motivated than Money Driven. Know the difference between Riches and Wealth, is that You can never be Wealthy, if you are only Money Driven and Money Motivated. Yes, You can be Rich, but you can not be Wealthy. But if you are Value Driven and Value motivated to make living life easy and better , for all, You will definitely become Wealthy in a matter of time.

RISK MANAGEMENT-

Risk management is the identification, assessment, and prioritization of risks (the effect of uncertainty on objectives) followed by coordinating and economical application of resources to minimize, monitor, and control the probability and impact of unfortunate events or to maximize the realization of opportunities. Risks can come from uncertainty in financial markets, threats from project failures (at any phase in the design, development, production, or sustainment life-cycles), legal liabilities, credit risk, accidents, natural causes and disasters as well as a deliberate attack from an adversary, or events of uncertain or unpredictable root-cause. Several risk management studies, like actuarial science is very important. Methods, definitions and goals vary widely according to whether the risk management method is in the context of project management, security, engineering, industrial processes, financial portfolios, actuarial assessments, or public health and safety.

The strategies to manage threats (uncertainties with negative consequences) typically include transferring the threat to another party, avoiding the threat, reducing the negative effect or probability of the threat, or even accepting some or all of the potential or actual consequences of a particular threat, and the opposites for opportunities (uncertain future states with benefits). The process of identification, analysis and either acceptance or mitigation of uncertainty in investment decision-making. Essentially, risk management occurs anytime an investor or fund manager analyzes and attempts to quantify the potential for losses in an investment and then takes the appropriate action (or inaction) given their investment objectives and risk tolerance. Inadequate risk management can result in severe consequences for companies as well as individuals. For example, the recession that began in 2008 was largely caused by the loose credit risk management of financial firms.

CHAPTER 14.

FINANCIAL STABILITY-

Financial Stability is your ability to Financially stand the test of time in the face of scarcity and uncertainties, The ability of your business to meet its debts as they fall due. Incase of emergency, You are not moved and unshaken. No financial needs meet you by surprise. You are able to conveniently pay your bills and purchase anything you need at anytime. Financial Stability is a level where you can afford anything money can buy, or a level where all your financial needs are taken care of. Financial Stability is when your assets surpass your liabilities. As an Individual, Corporation, Organization, Institution or Nation. Financial Stability is important and that's what we crave for. From the first day at work till the days of retiringment, we long for financial stability. My advice to you is, if you are not yet financially stable, don't ever retire. I tell people that, If you are tired don't retire, re-fire. If Warren Buffet, Chairman/CEO of Berkshire Hathaway INC, A Billionaire and One of the Top 3 Wealthiest Men in the World Still works at age 84, What's your excuse.

Why do you want to retire early. Fine You can retire or quit different jobs, but I will always advise people to build a career in line with their skills, passion, motivation and talent. Death is the only event that should make you retire. You are still battling to stabilize your credit, and you are already thinking of retirement. Don't be a burden to human existence. Be an addition to humanity. Contribute your own quota to human existence. Be a Creator, Lend a helping hand. Show your own support. Do something. You don't need someone to believe in you to be the best, You only need to believe in yourself to be the best. Check the list of Billionaires, You will see the list ranging from age 20's to 90. I believe Retirement is only applicable to employees, but the question is, do you want to be an employee all your life.

When do you want to be an employer. What the Wealthy Do, is that they Insure, instead of retire.

Financial stability to an Organization or a nation is a state in which the financial system, i.e. the key financial markets and the financial institutional system are resistant to economic shocks and is fit to smoothly fulfil its basic functions: the intermediation of financial funds, management of risks and the arrangement of payments.

BE GENEROUS-

What so ever you make happen for others, God will make happen for you. What so ever you do to others, will be done unto you. Givers never lack, and the more you give, the more you get, What you sow, you reap. The Wealthy are Generous Givers. The liberal soul shall be made fat. Prosperity is of the Soul. Before you start experiencing Wealth in the form of Financial Riches, You will first experience it in your soul. It starts from inside out. You must possess a large heart to Access Abundance Wealth. Giving and Generosity is very important, if you must be wealthy in life. God will never bless you, if you are not ready to release a fraction of what he has blessed you with. If you can't give out, you can never take in. In the same light, if God gives you an idea, what is the use, if you refuse to use it.

You can't be tight fisted, you must experience Blessings and Abundance. As a matter of truth, the Government cannot take care of everyone, the Responsibilities are too much. The World needs, more and more generous people, for the World to be a better place for all. Be Generous. Give without *stress, don't ever feel, you are loosing anytime you give. It's a Blessing to Give. As a matter of truth, It's more Blessed to Give than to receive. Now, giving as got nothing to do with your Possessions. Giving is of the heart. It's a lifestyle. I know that people have given their lives for the sake of humanity.*

I know people that laid down their lives for humanity. Let me quickly make clarity between, Assets and Possessions.

Their is a lot of misconception between What you own as Assets and What you have as Possessions. Often times, we think Our Houses, Cars, Private Yacht, Jet and some Properties are Assets. No, it's not. Anything you possess or own, that is not making you an extra income or bringing you Returns is not an Asset. It's a Liability Possession. If whatever you own is not making you money, then its Liability. If you own anything, and it's not making you money, then it's definitely taking resources away from you. You will need money, to maintain and manage, whatever possession you own, that's not making you money. Whatever you own as possessions, but yielding Returns for you is an Investment and that's an Asset.

If each one will reach one, then each one can live on. Living life is beyond existence, because if you are living without any meaningful impact in the lives of people around you, then you are just existing. This as got nothing to do with Money in the Bank or How rich you are. Do your best and leave the rest. showing a readiness to give more of something, as money or time, than is strictly necessary or expected. We all know about love, Now what is love, you may want to ask once again. I define love as simply Giving. The proof of Love is Giving. Check through history, about anyone that has claimed to Love, It shows through Giving. Givers Never Lack, and If you give bountifully, you will reap Bountifully, but if you give sparingly you will reap sparingly. Being Broke Sucks. The Moment you start thinking of what you can give, Your life will change forever. Life is more about what You can give, than what you can get. Don't Think of what you can get out of life, Think more about what you can Give. Give and it shall come back to you. The hand that gives will always remain on top. Always look for the slightest opportunity to give. You can give others your resources, like your time, knowledge, assistance and support when necessary, it's charity.

CHAPTER 15.

WEALTH MANAGEMENT-

Wealth management as an investment-advisory discipline incorporates financial planning, investment portfolio management and a number of aggregated financial services. High-net-worth individuals (HNWIs), small-business owners and families who desire the assistance of a credentialed financial advisory specialist, call upon wealth managers to coordinate retail banking, estate planning, legal resources, tax professionals and investment management. Wealth managers can have backgrounds as independent Chartered Financial Consultants, Certified Financial Planners or Chartered Financial Analysts (in the USA), Chartered Strategic Wealth Professionals (in Canada), Chartered Financial Planners (in the UK), or any credentials (such as an MBA) professional money managers who work to enhance the income, growth and tax-favored treatment of long-term investors. One must already have accumulated some amount of wealth for wealth management strategies to be effective. Historically the entry bar was high, however recently due to innovations such as exchange-traded funds, increased transparency in product design and more and more investors managing their own investments, this entry bar is coming down. However, several firms offer this service to minimum investments of $1M down to £100K.

THE LABOUR MARKET-

Your Job Search ends here. Unemployment is not the unavailability of jobs sometimes, but the lack of skills and competences for the growing trend of the available jobs, which can be a result of different factors like Technology, Technical Know How, Skill Acquisition, Wisdom, Knowledge, & Understanding, Training, Hands on Experience and Passion for the Job or Lack of Motivation. Self Development, Skill set, Expertise, Professionalism in terms of approach, Education (formal or informal knowledge), Information, Moral Values, Courtesy, Polite Behaviors, Mannerism, Work Ethics, can be the requirements to get certain jobs, ad these are the building blocks of our attitude. Your Attitude, they say determines your Altitude in life, 98% of employers, employ based on your good attitude to the job . Attitude is everything when it comes to success. Attitude is 98% of Success habits and 2% of hard work. In the workplace, we know that hard work as limitations, but attitude as no limitations. You can soar to the Highest Height of any Career in life with Good Attitude. Bad Attitude can ruin a million years of labor. Good attitude in life determines the flow of favor in your life. Your Attitude can make or mar you and your career. Good attitude can make you employable at anytime. I put this way. That, I have been hired for the best jobs I ever got, by my Attitude and not really because of my skills or knowledge. Whenever you see a situation whereby some people are getting hired just like that, check, they have a good attitude. An employer, will rather hire an employee for good attitude than for hard work. The Ingredients of Good Attitude are as follows, Responsibility, Accountability, Focus, Commitment, Sacrifice, Self Discipline, Humility, Respect, Love, Joy, Peace, Patience, Goodness, Kindness and Self Control. It has got nothing to do with being smart, and everything to do with Self Development.

A lot of people are growing, but they are not developing, we have often heard that age is just a number, Yes, lots of people are growing, but they are not developing. Self Development as got to do with maturity. It has nothing to do with your age. In the case of a Nation, Lot's of countries are growing but are not developing. They have a good economy, but the Standard of living of their citizens is extremely poor. Beautiful, High rise buildings, Good Road network, Strong Financial Institutions and Good Social Amenities, but the high cost of living with low earning power.

STAY FOCUSED -

Stop The Rat Race, Life is not a Race, Stay in your lane, Mind your Own Business, What works for you, might not work for your friend. No Competition.
Force of focus keeps everything into perspective to keep you on track per time. Focus keeps you single minded and on point at every point in time. Avoid Distractions. Live a focus driven life. A double minded individual is unstable in all ways. You can't be wealthy as a double minded individual. Discover your purpose, Stick to the plan. You can never Win, by running another person's race. Your purpose is strongly connected to your Talent, Passions and Motivation, these are clues to your purpose in life. When purpose is unknown, abuse is inevitable. Focus, get the job done easier, faster and better.

Let me use this illustration: If you are too close to an object, you will not see the right view, and if you are too far from an object, you will not see the right view, but if you must have a proper view of any object, you have to be standing at an accurate distance. Staying Focused gives you an accurate distance of Your Goals, in life. Distraction makes your goal far away from you, Desperation makes your goal too close to you, but Focus keeps you at an accurate distance.

SELF DISCIPLINE (SD)-

Delayed Gratification and Self Control are very strong building blocks for living your dream and staying wealthy. Your attitude determines your altitude. But how do you develop a strong attitude? You must have self control. The Stronger your self discipline, the better your attitude. Self Control, is a major building block to any height to achieving any level of success in any area of endeavor in life. The more you quench your taste for quick and instant pleasure. The better your chances of moving very close to your successful destination. Lots of multi-billion dollar corporations started in the garage. They never started in the penthouse of a sky scrapper. Multi- Billion Dollar corporations started from the bottom and were built and developed a very great height, built from a solid foundation. your ability to control your feelings and overcome your weaknesses, and the ability to pursue what you think is right despite temptations to abandon it. Self Discipline also means Training and control of oneself and one's conduct, usually for personal improvement or the act of disciplining or power to discipline one's own feelings and desires with the intention of improving oneself.

START SMALL-

It's difficult for a lot of people to start small, because of the commitment and dedication it requires. Self denial and Sacrifice is very important to start small. Procrastination as being linked to laziness and the negligence to start small. I always tell people to start from where they are, with what *they have. If you can't fly, then Run, If you can't Run, then Walk, If you can't Walk then Crawl, If you can't Crawl then Move. Don't ever remain Stagnant in Life, You are Programmed for Progress. We all know that the Stagnant water is a deadly breed of water borne diseases. If you are not progressive, you will soon be forgotten and left behind or become outdated and irrelevant. If you take in and you don't give out, you will soon become stinking just like stagnant water, you will breath toxic and become wasted.*

CHAPTER 16.

GOALS SETTING-

Start small but don't remain small, see the big picture and your great end in mind. Success is a Process, It's work in Progress. It's the building block for leaving your dream, don't just have big dreams, but live your dream. Don't watch your Dream turn into a Nightmare. Having Big Dreams without Working towards it, is like a disaster waiting to happen. You need to set Goals with Timeline, That's leaving your Dream. Faith without works is dead. Same way, Dreams Without Set Goals is a nightmare. If Wishes were horses Beggars will ride for free. Don't just be a wishful Thinker. Take Practical Steps towards making your dream a Reality. Never procrastinate, whatever is worth doing is worth doing well. Don't be idle, because the idle mind is the devil's workshop. Engage your mind in critical thinking. If you can think deep enough, you will discover a lasting solution to any situation confronting you. The solutions to your challenges is at the mercy of creative thinking. Nothing Is Impossible, only if you believe.

WILL POWER-

The strength of will to carry out one's decisions, wishes, or plans. Will power is the ability to control or restrain oneself. Always save the best for the last. If you eat your seed, You will be left with no harvest. I tell people, that if you play when others are working, You will work when others are playing. Always do the right thing at the right time. Seed time and Harvest, shall never cease. There's a time and a season for everything. It takes a strong will power to do the right thing. Sow your seed when its day time and never withhold your hands at night. Meaning, you have to keep sowing if you want to keep reaping, and you have to keep sowing if you want to always harvest. In Business Terms, You have to keep Investing If you always want Return on Investment.

However your life turns out, It's your own decision. You choose the quality of your own life. You become whatever you choose to become. If You Believe You Can, Yes You are Right and If You Believe you Can't, Yes! You are right. Yes or No, You Choose Your answer.

Sometimes in life, we all go through the same situations, challenges and conditions, but some people choose to remain drowned in their situations while others take the bull by the horn, stand tall to their challenge, look it in the face and say No way, I will conquer. The global financial crisis is obvious in the World, but the truth is that, some people are rising high in the face of the meltdown, while others are crying out for help. The Financial Crisis is a stepping stone for some, while it stands as a stumbling block for others. You choose where you desire to be in life, either on the Mountain Top or at the Bottom Valley. It's your choice if you decide to remain in the street or move up to the suite. For every stumbling block, there is a stepping stone. Every disappointment is a Blessing. I said before, that Anywhere there is Scarcity, Abundance is available somewhere else. It's up to you to decide where you belong. You can either be an at an advantage or disadvantage, it's up to you.

THE EAGLE-

The Eagle stands out in all species of birds available in the World. Whenever there is heavy storm or wind, other birds take cover or run to their shelter, but that is when the Eagle soars high in the sky. The Eagle pitch it's nest on The Mountain Top. Many times, in order to survive, we have to start a change process. We sometimes need to get rid of old memories, habits and other past traditions. Only freed from past burdens, can we take advantage of the present.

COMMITMENT-

No one is born to remain at the bottom. Everyone desires to be at the top, but why is everyone not at the top, it's simply because of choices we make consciously or unconsciously on daily bases. Every one desires to be rich, but why is everyone not rich, it's simply because of our choices. We have heard of stories of people that rose from rag to riches, from the ghetto to glory and from grass to grace. This can happen to anyone, anywhere in the world.

DEDICATION-

Your life today, is a reflection and a result of what you have dedicated your time to doing, in the past. Nothing in life happens by chance, Nothing happens by accident. Your life today is the outcome of your past input. If you want a brighter future, then dedicate your time to more productive lifestyle. No excuse for failure, failure is not an option, Yes, you may fall, but don't remain on the ground. Get Up!

SACRIFICE-

I sometimes, call sacrifice alternative forgone. Sacrifice is letting go, of whatever gives you temporary satisfaction, in place what will give you permanent success in the future, which is somewhat difficult to do. You are giving up temporary, on what will give way to an opportunity of a lifetime. Sacrifice is one of the major Success and Rich Habits.

We all love the good things of life and we all want to live the kind of lifestyle we desire, but only a few are ready to sacrifice the temporary, present enjoyment, for a well deserved future, they desire. Good Cars, Houses, Jewelries Clothes, Shoes and personal belonging is what we all want, but only few can spare a couple of dollars to buy constructive and successful books and get a good knowledge on what will change their lives and make their lives better. Did you know, that the same amount you spend on a combo food pack and a drink, Can get you a book at the same price, that will change your life forever? Sometimes, the money people spend on liquor, beer, smoking and pleasure, is much more than what they will spend on buying a book, to improve their lives and Transform their lives forever. Change is the only constant thing in life, but change doesn't come by chance, It comes from deliberate practical practice, the desire and the readiness for change. In most cases, a lot of people are forced to change. Suddenly the unexpected happens and they have no choice but to go with the flow and change with the situation. But you don't have to be forced to change. Don't wait until the expected change your life. Bring the Change you so much desire, into your own life. Never quench your quest for change, It is worth a lifetime of Billion Dollars. Sometimes, change happens and some people are not even aware, and before they realize what happened, they are already carried away in the frenzy. The Internet changed the World, globally, in the wake of the new millennium, and turned the world into a global village, before people know what was going on, it has taken over our lives. The World became a Global Village, and now with the advent of the social media, I call the World a "Control Room". Now people know, what's happening anywhere in the World, real time. Your family, friend and enemies now know your daily to do list and they can predict what you are up to on a daily bases. People can easily tell, where you are and what you have been up to lately.

At 16, he was able to save a little more for himself shortly after high school, looking forward to a bright future to gain admission into one of the Ivies. Then he thought to himself, what he could use his savings to purchase for himself, a wonderful treasured possession will be a good idea, he thought to himself, looking at what his friends and peer group, are buying with their savings after high school. An expensive bike, motor cycle, skateboard, go shopping in one of the finest boutiques in town to buy clothes and shoes , go to a driving school to learn how to drive, buy a fine jewelry, different ideas flowed through his mind. At some point he became confused, and had no idea, what to do with his savings. While In his thought, one day, he came across an old book on the coffee table, the book has been lying there for days, dropped by his dad. He flipped through the pages, and he learned a couple of knowledge. Then he thought to himself, why don't I use my savings to buy books. That was it. He decided to use his savings to buy books. He woke the next morning, and he went straight to the bookshops in town, to purchase books on self development and self help, in Finance, Business, Relationships, Knowledge, Technology, Mind Development, Investment, etc. At 19 he started his own company, by buying shares in multinational corporations, Ten years later, he became a Millionaire with Interest in major businesses. To be master, you must be reader, Readers are Learners and Learners are Teachers. Attitude is Everything. Humility, Loyalty and Respect. These are the habits of the Rich, Your Attitude determines your Altitude.

CHAPTER 17.

PERSISTENCE & CONSISTENCE.

Constant Practice, is What Makes you perfect in anything you desire and your area of Specialization. Practice Makes Perfect.

Determination- Failure is not an option, You have no excuse for failure, You can never look back and predict your future. You've got to press on. Be a Goal Getter, Go for it. Keep Pushing- Encourage, Motivate and Push Yourself, Take Action, Do Something. Never Procrastinate, It terminates your motivation. We say Procrastination is the assassination and the elimination of your motivation-Never be afraid to fail, face your fears, Try again, you must have learnt from your mistakes. It's time to move on, It's a new day, stand up, brush yourself and move forward.

GET A COACH-

YOU need a MENTOR.
Can you imagine an athlete without a coach? That's why you need a

mentor. To stay rich, you must have a mentor to understudy his/her principles of success. I have several mentors in different endeavor . It's a wise choice. Have you ever met a student without a tutor? You need to get a mentor. Someone you desire to be like, someone you cherish their success. Someone who can mentor or tutor you. Mentorship is crucial to your success. Can you imagine children without parents? Your mentor will be your guide and they can give you direction. Mentors are like indicators and pointers to direct you all the way to your successful destination.

A Heart Desire to be Rich.
See Your Big Future-Your Mental Picture is your Actual Future.
Imagination is Your Potential Talent, Use it to your advantage. Mind Power.
Don't Quench your Quest- Never Give Up.Don't Give in on yourself, Don't Quit on your dreams. Be Strong, Be Courageous and Keep Hope Alive. Quitters never win.

Self Worth-

Your Self-worth determines your Net Worth. Self Confidence, High Self Esteem. Boldness and Courage. Bravery and Strong Will.
Game Plan. Insanity is doing the same thing same way and expecting a different result.
The Good News is reading "The Money Book" Guarantee's you a Better Chance of Getting Rich and as often as you read this book, you have a chance of getting Richer only if you take action on what you learn from it. Anyone can be rich at any time. But not everyone can stay rich, meaning not everyone can Stay Rich!. Anyone can become successful at any time, but not everyone can Remain Successful. That's where this book comes in, and it will be very important in your life. This Smart book will help you

develop Financial prudence, will teach you Financial intelligence, How you can Maintain Your Riches, and pass it on to your next Generation, How you can build a Wealth Legacy and a Prosperous Empire, You Will Know everything about Financial Freedom or Liberty and you will be Armed Passion with Financial Knowledge. If you succeed or fail, you take the credit or blame. No one else will. Success has many fathers, but failure has none. No one will ever want to identify with failure. Dare to Succeed. Revenge your haters and enemies with your success.

This Rich Book will teach you What Smart People do. The Richest don't own everything, but can afford anything money can buy. The Common Thing about The Rich is That They are Money Smart They may not be Book Smart, But They Work smart and they are Street Smart.
In this Smart Book, you will know what it means to be Money Smart, Street Smart, Book Smart, Work Smart, Think Smart, Live Smart, How Smart People Think, What Smart People do, The Smart Age, Smart Generation, The Smart Guy, The Smart Lady. You Will Realize There's nothing new under heaven. You ain't smart till you have a proof, you don't have to prove it. Smart People don't prove it, They have proofs.

Smart Choice, Time and Money Management, Smart Investment, Smart Spending, Work Smarter not Harder, The Good news is, There's room for improvement, The Bad news is Sitting around and doing nothing.
Let me tell you the reason why there are so many poor people in the world. The rich are generous givers, yet they get richer, the poor hardly give yet they get poorer. The Rich always plant and sow their seed, this means the rich always invest their money and resources, that's the reason they always get richer, but the poor always eat their seed, meaning they spend always,

thats the reason for their poverty.If you invest your money, you can always expect Return on Investment but if you spend your money, you have successfully helped the investor get richer and you gain instant gratification that soon ends in a couple of minutes or hours.

You don't have to know everything to get rich, you don't have to own everything to get rich, you don't need all the money in the world to get rich but you need to be wise and money smart to Stay Rich.

SMART NEGOTIATION & BARGAINING-

The terms and conditions of a transaction. Bargaining is a type of negotiation in which the buyer and seller of a good or service debate the price and exact nature of a transaction. If the bargaining produces agreement on terms, the transaction takes place. Bargaining is an alternative pricing strategy to fix prices Optimally, if it costs the retailer nothing to engage and allow bargaining, he can divine the buyer's willingness to spend. It allows for capturing more consumer discipline as it allows price discrimination, a process whereby a seller can charge a higher price to one buyer who is more eager (by being richer or more desperate). Haggling has largely disappeared in parts of the world where the cost to haggle exceeds the gain to retailers for most common retail items. However, for expensive goods sold to uninformed buyers such as automobiles, bargaining can remain commonplace.

CHAPTER 18.

Call the shorts,

Mind your own business, nobody's business.The Money Smart are the Investors.

Warren Edward Buffett (born August 30, 1930) is an American business magnate, investor, and philanthropist. He is widely considered the most successful investor of the 20th century. Buffett is the chairman, CEO and largest shareholder of Berkshire Hathaway and consistently ranked among the world's wealthiest people. He was ranked as the world's wealthiest person in 2008 and as the third wealthiest person in 2011. In 2012, American magazine Time named Buffett one of the most influential people in the world. Buffett is called the "Wizard of Omaha", "Oracle of Omaha", or the "Sage of Omaha"and is noted for his adherence to the value investing philosophy and for his personal frugality despite his immense wealth. Buffett is also a notable philanthropist, having pledged to give away 99 percent of his fortune to philanthropic causes, primarily via the Gates Foundation. On April 11, 2012, he was diagnosed with prostate cancer,for which he successfully completed treatment in September 2012.

Buffett was born in 1930 in Omaha, Nebraska, the second of three children and only son of U.S. congressman Howard Buffett,a fierce critic of the interventionist New Deal domestic and foreign policy, and his wife Leila (née Stahl). Buffett's DNA report revealed that his paternal ancestors hail from northern Scandinavia, while his maternal ancestors hail from Iberia (present-day Spain) or Estonia.

Buffett began his education at Rose Hill Elementary School in Omaha. In 1942, his father was elected to the first of four terms in the United States Congress, and after moving with his family to Washington, D.C., Warren finished elementary school, attended Alice Deal Junior High School, and graduated from Woodrow Wilson High School in 1947, where his senior yearbook picture reads: "likes math; a future stockbroker".
Even as a child, Buffett displayed an interest in making and saving money. He went door to door selling chewing gum, Coca-Cola, or weekly magazines. For a while, he worked in his grandfather's grocery store. While still in high school, he was successful in making money by delivering newspapers, selling golf balls and stamps, and detailing cars, among other means. Filing his first income tax return in 1944, Buffett took a $35 deduction for the use of his bicycle and watch on his paper route. In 1945, in his sophomore year of high school, Buffett and a friend spent $25 to purchase a used pinball machine, which they placed in the local barber shop. Within months, they owned several machines in different barber shops.
Buffett's interest in the stock market and investing also dated to his childhood, to the days he spent in the customers' lounge of a regional

stock brokerage near the office of his father's own brokerage company. On a trip to New York City at the age of ten, he made a point to visit the New York Stock Exchange. At the age of 11, he bought three shares of Cities Service Preferred for himself, and three for his sister. While in high school, he invested in a business owned by his father and bought a farm worked by a tenant farmer.

Buffett entered college as a freshman in 1947 at the Wharton School of the University of Pennsylvania. He studied there for two years and joined the Alpha Sigma Phi fraternity. He then transferred to the University of Nebraska–Lincoln where at the age of nineteen, he graduated with a Bachelor of Science in business administration.

After being rejected by Harvard Business School, Buffett enrolled at Columbia Business School after learning that Benjamin Graham (author of "The Intelligent Investor" – one of his favorite books on investing) and David Dodd, two well-known securities analysts, taught there. He earned a Master of Science in economics from Columbia in 1951. Buffett also attended the New York Institute of Finance.

Buffett was employed from 1951 to 1954 at Buffett-Falk & Co., Omaha as an investment salesman; from 1954 to 1956 at Graham-Newman Corp., New York as a securities analyst; from 1956 to 1969 at Buffett Partnership, Ltd., Omaha as a general partner; and from 1970 – present at Berkshire Hathaway Inc, Omaha as its Chairman, CEO.

In 1950, at the age of 20, Buffett had made and saved $9,800 (over $96,000 inflation adjusted for the 2014 USD). In April 1952, Buffett discovered Graham was on the board of GEICO insurance. Taking a train to Washington, D.C. on a Saturday, he knocked on the door of GEICO's headquarters until a janitor allowed him in. There he met Lorimer Davidson, Geico's Vice President, and the two discussed the insurance business for hours. Davidson would eventually become Buffett's lifelong friend and a lasting influence and later recall that he found Buffett to be an *"extraordinary man" after only fifteen minutes. Buffett graduated from Columbia and wanted to work on Wall Street, however, both his father and Ben Graham urged him not to. He offered to work for Graham for free, but Graham refused.*

Buffett returned to Omaha and worked as a stockbroker while taking a Dale Carnegie public speaking course. Using what he learned, he felt confident enough to teach an "Investment Principles" night class at the University of Nebraska-Omaha. The average age of his students was more than twice his own. During this time he also purchased a Sinclair Texaco gas station as a side investment. However, this did not turn out to be a successful business venture.[citation needed]

In 1952,[28] Buffett married Susan Thompson at Dundee Presbyterian Church and the next year they had their first child, Susan Alice Buffett. In 1954, Buffett accepted a job at Benjamin Graham's partnership. His starting salary was $12,000 a year (approximately $105,000 inflation adjusted for the 2012 USD). There he worked closely with Walter Schloss. Graham was a tough man to work for. He was adamant that stocks provide a wide margin of safety after weighting the trade-off between their price and their intrinsic value. The argument made sense to Buffett but he questioned whether the criteria were too stringent and caused the company to miss out on big winners that had more qualitative values.[citation needed] That same year the Buffetts had their second child, Howard Graham Buffett. In 1956, Benjamin Graham retired and closed his partnership. At this time Buffett's personal savings were over $174,000 ($1.47 million inflation adjusted to 2012 USD and he started Buffett Partnership Ltd., an investment partnership in Omaha.

CHAPTER 19.

In 1957, Buffett had three partnerships operating the entire year. He
purchased a five-bedroom stucco house in Omaha, where he still lives, for
$31,500. In 1958 the Buffetts' third child, Peter Andrew Buffett, was born.
Buffett operated five partnerships the entire year. In 1959, the company
grew to six partnerships operating the entire year and Buffett was
introduced to Charlie Munger. By 1960, Buffett had seven partnerships
operating: Buffett Associates, Buffett Fund, Dacee, Emdee, Glenoff, Mo-Buff
and Underwood. He asked one of his partners, a doctor, to find ten other
doctors willing to invest $10,000 each in his partnership. Eventually eleven
agreed, and Buffett pooled their money with a mere $100 original
investment of his own. In 1961, Buffett revealed that the Sanborn Map
Company accounted for 35% of the partnership's assets. He explained that
in 1958 Sanborn stock sold for only $45 per share when the value of the
Sanborn investment portfolio was $65 per share. This meant that buyers
valued Sanborn stock at "minus $20" per share and were unwilling to pay

more than 70 cents on the dollar for an investment portfolio with a map business thrown in for nothing. This earned him a spot on the board of Sanborn.

As a millionaire

In 1962, Buffett became a millionaire because of his partnerships, which in January 1962 had an excess of $7,178,500, of which over $1,025,000 belonged to Buffett. Buffett merged all partnerships into one partnership. Buffett invested in and eventually took control of a textile manufacturing firm, Berkshire Hathaway. In 1962, Warren Buffett began buying shares in Berkshire from Seabury Stanton, the owner, whom he later fired. Buffett's partnerships began purchasing shares at $7.60 per share. In 1965, when Buffett's partnerships began purchasing Berkshire aggressively, they paid $14.86 per share while the company had working capital of $19 per share. This did not include the value of fixed assets (factory and equipment).

Buffett took control of Berkshire Hathaway at the board meeting and named a new president, Ken Chace, to run the company. In 1966, Buffett closed the partnership to new money. He would go on to claim that the textile business had been his worst trade.[29] He then moved the business into the insurance sector, and, in 1985, the last of the mills that had been the core business of Berkshire Hathaway was sold. Buffett wrote in his letter: "... unless it appears that circumstances have changed (under some conditions added capital would improve results) or unless new partners can bring some asset to the partnership other than simply capital, I intend to admit no additional partners to BPL."

In a second letter, Buffett announced his first investment in a private business — Hochschild, Kohn and Co, a privately owned Baltimore department store. In 1967, Berkshire paid out its first and only dividend of 10 cents. In 1969, following his most successful year, Buffett liquidated the partnership and transferred their assets to his partners. Among the assets paid out were shares of Berkshire Hathaway. In 1970, as chairman of Berkshire Hathaway, Buffett began writing his now-famous annual letters to shareholders. However, he lived solely on his salary of $50,000 per year, and his outside investment income. In 1979, Berkshire began the year trading at $775 per share, and ended at $1,310. Buffett's net worth reached $620 million, placing him on the Forbes 400 for the first time.

In 1973, Berkshire began to acquire stock in the Washington Post Company. Buffett became close friends with Katharine Graham, who controlled the company and its flagship newspaper, and became a member of its board of directors. In 1974, the SEC opened a formal investigation into Warren Buffett and Berkshire's acquisition of WESCO, due to possible conflict of interest. No charges were brought. In 1977, Berkshire indirectly purchased the Buffalo Evening News for $32.5 million. Antitrust charges started, instigated by its rival, the Buffalo Courier-Express. Both papers lost money, until the Courier-Express folded in 1982.

In 1979, Berkshire began to acquire stock in ABC.

Capital Cities announced $3.5 billion purchase of ABC on March 18, 1985 surprised the media industry, as ABC was four times bigger than Capital Cities at the time. Berkshire Hathaway chairman Warren Buffett helped finance the deal in return for a 25% stake in the combined company.The newly merged company, known as Capital Cities/ABC (or CapCities/ABC), was forced to sell off some stations due to FCC ownership rules. Also, the two companies owned several radio stations in the same markets

In 1987, Berkshire Hathaway purchased a 12% stake in Salomon Inc., making it the largest shareholder and Buffett the director. In 1990, a scandal involving John Gutfreund (former CEO of Salomon Brothers) surfaced. A rogue trader, Paul Mozer, was submitting bids in excess of what was allowed by the Treasury rules. When this was discovered and brought to the attention of Gutfreund, he did not immediately suspend the rogue trader. Gutfreund left the company in August 1991.Buffett became Chairman of Salomon until the crisis passed; on September 4, 1991, he testified before Congress.

In 1988, Buffett began buying stock in Coca-Cola Company, eventually purchasing up to 7% of the company for $1.02 billion. It would turn out to *be one of Berkshire's most lucrative investments, and one which it still holds.*

As a billionaire

CHAPTER 20.

Buffett became a billionaire on paper when Berkshire Hathaway began selling class A shares on May 29, 1990, with the market closing at US$7,175 a share. In 1998 he acquired General Re (Gen Re) as a subsidiary in a deal that presented difficulties for Buffett from the outset—according the Rational Walk investment website, "underwriting standards proved to be inadequate," while a "problematic derivatives book" was resolved after numerous years and a significant loss. Gen Re later provided reinsurance after Buffett became involved with Maurice R. Greenberg at AIG in 2002.

During a 2005 investigation of an accounting fraud case involving AIG, a number of Gen Re executives became implicated. On March 15, 2005, the AIG board forced Greenberg to resign from his post as Chairman and CEO after regulators believed that AIG engaged in questionable transactions and improper accounting.On February 9, 2006, AIG and the New York State Attorney General's office agreed to a settlement over the fraud case that required AIG to pay a fine of US$1.6 billion. In 2010 the federal U.S. government agreed to a US$92 million settlement with Gen Re, meaning that the Berkshire Hathaway subsidiary would avoid prosecution in the AIG case. Gen Re also made a commitment to implement "corporate governance concessions," which required Berkshire Hathaway's Chief Financial Officer to attend General Re's audit committee meetings and mandated the appointment of an independent director.

In 2002, Buffett entered in US$11 billion worth of forward contracts to deliver U.S. dollars against other currencies. By April 2006, his total gain on these contracts was over US$2 billion. In 2006, Buffett announced in June that he gradually would give away 85% of his Berkshire holdings to five foundations in annual gifts of stock, starting in July 2006—the largest contribution would go to the Bill and Melinda Gates Foundation.

In 2007, in a letter to shareholders, Buffett announced that he was looking for a younger successor, or perhaps successors, to run his investment business. Buffett had previously selected Lou Simpson, who runs investments at Geico, to fill the role; however, Simpson is only six years younger than Buffett.

On 14 August 2014, the price of Berkshire Hathaway's shares hit US $200,000 a share for the first time, capitalizing the company at US$328 billion. While Buffett had given away much of his stock to charities by this time, he still held 321,000 shares worth US$64.2 billion.

On 20 August 2014, Berkshire Hathaway was fined $896,000 for failing to report the 9 December 2013 purchase of shares in USG Corporation as required.

CHAPTER 21.

Desire to be Rich.

See the Big Picture, Your Big Future-Your Mental Picture is your Actual Future...Imagination is Your Potential Talent, Use it to your advantage. Mind Power.

Never Give Up.Don't Give en on yourself, don't give up on your dreams. Be Strong, Be Courageous and Keep Hope Alive. Quitters never win.

Time They Say is Money...Manage your time wisely never Waste Time, Its the Greatest Resource of Mankind, It's Never Too Late, You can Start Afresh or Change Your Game Plan...Insanity is doing the same thing same way and expect a different result.

You can Make Mistakes But Don't Make Excuses, It Can Be Costly-

Mistakes can sometimes be costly. Years of labor can be destroyed overnight by just a simple stupid mistake. Same way, years of labor can turn around to Abundance, by a simple act of favor. Have you ever heard a medical doctor or a surgeon, give a report on Health issues or surgery operations, that, "Oh, and there was a slight mistake in the procedure? Oh, we made a slight mistake by placing the liver, where the kidney ought to be? You can't afford to make mistakes at the level of becoming successful in life and living your dream in life. You don't have a second chance to make the first impression in Life.
Can you go for a job interview , crucial to stepping up on your career ladder , and you walk into the interview like you are heading to a party? No. You need to dress to impress, to the corporate presentation.

You dress to impress. Even some night clubs will not give you entry and admission if you are not well dressed, not to talk about something of importance. You can lose the interest of a client simply because of your dress sense.

Some common mistakes have ruined some people's lives, that's why they say common sense is not common. Some people have said the wrong things at the wrong time. Some have been found in the wrong place. Some people have fallen from Grace to Grass for wrong actions. Wisdom is the correct application of the Knowledge Understood. True! I say There is a Thin line between Wisdom and Foolishness and Which ever you display at every time (t) determines who you are. Wisdom is a display of our attitude every point in time, at our own discretion. If a Wise man does anything foolish at any point in time, He will be considered a foolish man, and If a foolish man appears to act wisely, he is considered a wise man. Wisdom and Foolishness walk side by side, we choose and decide, which one we want to live in accordance with. People make excuses whenever they act stupid or do anything foolish. Don't ever be caught in that web. It's very unattractive. It repels good fortunes. If you make mistakes, take responsibilities, and make amends where necessary, and promise yourself never to make such mistakes again. Imagine you sit for an examination to move on to the next class or a higher pedestal either in school or at work, and you make a mistake in answering the right questions. You can ruin the years, months, weeks, days and hours of your study and hard work, simply by that mistake which can grossly affect your life in the near future. I know people that are perceived as genius, that became a nuisance, simply by making a simple mistake. Ignorance is never an excuse in life. You can ever prepare for battle on the battlefield if you must win. No one prepares for battle on the Battle Field, that's why Proper Preparations will always prevent poor performance in life. Live Prepared, Be Prepared and Be Ready always.

CHAPTER 22.

J.K ROWLING.

Joanne "Jo" Rowling, (born 31 July 1965), pen names J. K. Rowling and Robert Galbraith, is a British novelist best known as the author of the Harry Potter fantasy series. The books have gained worldwide attention, won multiple awards, and sold more than 400 million copies. They have become the best-selling book series in history and been the basis for a series of films which became the highest-grossing film series in history. Rowling had overall approval on the scripts and maintained creative control by serving as a producer on the final instalment.

Born in Yate, Gloucestershire, Rowling was working as a researcher and bilingual secretary for Amnesty International when she conceived the idea for the Harry Potter series on a delayed train from Manchester to London in 1990.The seven-year period that followed saw the death of her mother, divorce from her first husband and relative poverty until Rowling finished the first novel in the series, Harry Potter and the Philosopher's Stone in 1997. There were six sequels, the last, Harry Potter and the Deathly Hallows in 2007. Since then, Rowling has written three books for adult readers, The Casual Vacancy (2012) and—under the pseudonym Robert Galbraith—the crime fiction novels The Cuckoo's Calling (2013) and The Silkworm (2014).

Rowling has led a "rags to riches" life story, in which she progressed from living on state benefits to multi-millionaire status within five years. She is the United Kingdom's best-selling living author, with sales in excess of £238m. The 2008 Sunday Times Rich List estimated Rowling's fortune at £560 million, ranking her as the twelfth richest woman in the United Kingdom. Forbes ranked Rowling as the forty-eighth most powerful celebrity of 2007, and Time magazine named her as a runner-up for its 2007 Person of the Year, noting the social, moral, and political inspiration she has given her fans. In October 2010, Rowling was named the "Most Influential Woman in Britain" by leading magazine editors. She has supported charities including Comic Relief, One Parent Families, Multiple Sclerosis Society of Great Britain and Lumos (formerly the Children's High Level Group), and in politics supports the Labour Party and Better Together.

Rowling was born to Peter James Rowling, a Rolls-Royce aircraft engineer, and Anne Rowling (née Volant), a science technician, on 31 July 1965 in Yate, Gloucestershire, England, 10 miles (16 km) northeast of Bristol. Her parents first met on a train departing from King's Cross Station bound for Arbroath in 1964. They married on 14 March 1965. One of her maternal great-grandfathers, Dugald Campbell, was Scottish, born in Lamlash on the Isle of Arran. Her mother's paternal grandfather, Louis Volant, was French, and was awarded the Croix de Guerre for exceptional bravery in defending the village of Courcelles-le-Comte during the First World War.

Rowling originally believed he had won the Légion d'honneur during the war, as she said when she received it herself in 2009. She later discovered the truth when featuring in an episode of the UK genealogy series Who Do You Think You Are?

Rowling's sister Dianne was born at their home when Rowling was 23 months old. The family moved to the nearby village Winterbourne when Rowling was four. She attended St Michael's Primary School, a school founded by abolitionist William Wilberforce and education reformer Hannah More. Her headmaster at St Michael's, Alfred Dunn, has been suggested as the inspiration for the Harry Potter headmaster Albus Dumbledore.

Rowling's childhood home, Church Cottage, Tutshill.- As a child, Rowling often wrote fantasy stories which she frequently read to her sister. Aged nine, Rowling moved to Church Cottage in the Gloucestershire village of Tutshill, close to Chepstow, Wales. She attended secondary school at Wyedean School and College, where her mother worked in the science department. When she was a young teenager, her great aunt gave her a copy of Jessica Mitford's autobiography, Hons and Rebels. Mitford became Rowling's heroine, and Rowling read all of her books.

Rowling has said that her teenage years were unhappy. Her home life was complicated by her mother's illness and a strained relationship with her father who she is still not on speaking terms with. Rowling later said that she based the character of Hermione Granger on herself when she was eleven. Steve Eddy, who taught Rowling English when she first arrived, remembers her as "not exceptional" but "one of a group of girls who were bright, and quite good at English". Sean Harris, her best friend in the Upper Sixth, owned a turquoise Ford Anglia which she says inspired a flying version that appeared in Harry Potter and the Chamber of Secrets. At this time, she listened to the Smiths and the Clash. Rowling took A-levels in English, French and German, achieving two A's and a B and was Head Girl.

In 1982, Rowling took the entrance exams for Oxford University but was not accepted and read for a BA in French and Classics at the University of Exeter. Martin Sorrell, a French professor at Exeter, remembers "a quietly competent student, with a denim jacket and dark hair, who, in academic terms, gave the appearance of doing what was necessary". Rowling recalls doing little work, preferring to listen to the Smiths and read Dickens and Tolkien. After a year of study in Paris, Rowling graduated from Exeter in 1986 and moved to London to work as a researcher and bilingual secretary for Amnesty International.

In 1988, Rowling wrote a short essay about her time studying Classics entitled "What was the Name of that Nymph Again? or Greek and Roman Studies Recalled"; it was published by the University of Exeter's journal Pegasus. Inspiration and mother's death.

CHAPTER 23.

After working at Amnesty International in London, Rowling and her then boyfriend decided to move to Manchester where she worked at the Chamber of Commerce. In 1990, while she was on a four-hour-delayed train trip from Manchester to London, the idea for a story of a young boy attending a school of wizardry "came fully formed" into her mind.

When she had reached her Clapham Junction flat, she began to write immediately. In December, Rowling's mother Anne died after ten years suffering from multiple sclerosis. Rowling was writing Harry Potter at the time and had never told her mother about it. Her death heavily affected Rowling's writing and she introduced much more detail about Harry's loss in the first book, because she knew how it felt.

Rowling moved to Porto to teach. In 1993, she returned to the UK accompanied by her daughter and three completed chapters of Harry Potter after her marriage had deteriorated. An advert in The Guardian led Rowling to move to Porto in Portugal to teach English as a foreign language. She taught at night, and began writing in the day while listening to Tchaikovsky's Violin Concerto.

After eighteen months in Porto, she met Portuguese television journalist Jorge Arantes in a bar, and found they shared an interest in Jane Austen. They married on 16 October 1992 and their child, Jessica Isabel Rowling Arantes (named after Jessica Mitford), was born on 27 July 1993 in Portugal. Rowling had previously suffered a miscarriage. The couple separated on 17 November 1993. Biographers have suggested that Rowling suffered domestic abuse during her marriage, although the full extent is unknown. In December 1993, Rowling and her daughter moved to be near Rowling's sister in Edinburgh, Scotland, with three chapters of Harry Potter in her suitcase.

Seven years after graduating from university, Rowling saw herself as a failure. Her marriage had failed, and she was jobless with a dependent child, but she described her failure as liberating and allowing her to focus on writing. During this period Rowling was diagnosed with clinical depression and contemplated suicide. Her illness inspired the characters known as Dementors, soul-sucking creatures introduced in the third book. Rowling signed up for welfare benefits, describing her economic status as being "poor as it is possible to be in modern Britain, without being homeless".

Rowling was left in despair after her estranged husband arrived in Scotland, seeking both her and her daughter. She obtained an order of restraint and Arantes returned to Portugal, with Rowling filing for divorce in August 1994.

She began a teacher training course in August 1995 at the Moray House School of Education, at Edinburgh University, after completing her first novel while living on state benefits. She wrote in many cafés, especially Nicolson's Café, and The Elephant House, (the former owned by her brother-in-law Roger Moore) wherever she could get Jessica to fall asleep. In a 2001 BBC interview, Rowling denied the rumour that she wrote in local cafés to escape from her unheated flat, pointing out that it had heating. One of the reasons she wrote in cafés was that taking her baby out for a walk was the best way to make her fall asleep.

CHAPTER 24.

"The Elephant House" – one of the cafés in Edinburgh in which Rowling wrote the first Harry Potter novel.

In 1995, Rowling finished her manuscript for Harry Potter and the Philosopher's Stone on an old manual typewriter. Upon the enthusiastic response of Bryony Evens, a reader who had been asked to review the book's first three chapters, the Fulham-based Christopher Little Literary Agents agreed to represent Rowling in her quest for a publisher. The book was submitted to twelve publishing houses, all of which rejected the manuscript. A year later she was finally given the green light (and a £1500 advance) by editor Barry Cunningham from Bloomsbury, a publishing house in London. The decision to publish Rowling's book owes much to Alice Newton, the eight-year-old daughter of Bloomsbury's chairman, who was given the first chapter to review by her father and immediately demanded the next. Although Bloomsbury agreed to publish the book, Cunningham says that he advised Rowling to get a day job, since she had little chance of making money in children's books. Soon after, in 1997, Rowling received an £8000 grant from the Scottish Arts Council to enable her to continue writing.

In June 1997, Bloomsbury published Philosopher's Stone with an initial print run of 1,000 copies, 500 of which were distributed to libraries. Today, such copies are valued between £16,000 and £25,000.

Five months later, the book won its first award, a Nestlé Smarties Book Prize. In February, the novel won the British Book Award for Children's Book of the Year, and later, the Children's Book Award. In early 1998, an auction was held in the United States for the rights to publish the novel, and was won by Scholastic Inc., for US$105,000. Rowling said that she "nearly died" when she heard the news. In October 1998, Scholastic published Philosopher's Stone in the US under the title of Harry Potter and the Sorcerer's Stone, a change Rowling says she now regrets and would have fought if she had been in a better position at the time. Rowling moved from her flat with the money from the Scholastic sale, into 19 Hazelbank Terrace in Edinburgh. Her neighbours were initially unaware that she was the author of the Harry Potter series, but treated her with respect.

Its sequel, Harry Potter and the Chamber of Secrets, was published in July 1998 and again Rowling won the Smarties Prize. In December 1999, the third novel, Harry Potter and the Prisoner of Azkaban, won the Smarties Prize, making Rowling the first person to win the award three times running. She later withdrew the fourth Harry Potter novel from contention to allow other books a fair chance. In January 2000, Prisoner of Azkaban won the inaugural Whitbread Children's Book of the Year award, though it lost the Book of the Year prize to Seamus Heaney's translation of Beowulf.

The fourth book, Harry Potter and the Goblet of Fire, was released simultaneously in the UK and the US on 8 July 2000 and broke sales records in both countries. 372,775 copies of the book were sold in its first day in the UK, almost equalling the number Prisoner of Azkaban sold during its first year. In the US, the book sold three million copies in its first 48 hours, smashing all records. Rowling said that she had had a crisis while writing the novel and had to rewrite one chapter many times to fix a problem with the plot. Rowling was named Author of the Year in the 2000 British Book Awards.

A wait of three years occurred between the release of Goblet of Fire and the fifth Harry Potter novel, Harry Potter and the Order of the Phoenix. This gap led to press speculation that Rowling had developed writer's block, speculations she denied. Rowling later said that writing the book was a chore, that it could have been shorter, and that she ran out of time and energy as she tried to finish it.

CHAPTER 25.

The sixth book, Harry Potter and the Half-Blood Prince, was released on 16 July

2005. It too broke all sales records, selling nine million copies in its first 24 hours

of release. In 2006, Half-Blood Prince received the Book of the Year prize at the

British Book Awards.

The title of the seventh and final Harry Potter book was announced on 21

December 2006 as Harry Potter and the Deathly Hallows. In February 2007 it was

reported that Rowling wrote on a bust in her hotel room at the Balmoral Hotel in

Edinburgh that she had finished the seventh book in that room on 11 January

2007. Harry Potter and the Deathly Hallows was released on 21 July 2007 (0:01

BST) and broke its predecessor's record as the fastest-selling book of all time. It

sold 11 million copies in the first day of release in the United Kingdom and United

States. The book's last chapter was one of the earliest things she wrote in the entire series.

Harry Potter is now a global brand worth an estimated US$15 billion, and the last four Harry Potter books have consecutively set records as the fastest-selling books in history. The series, totalling 4,195 pages, has been translated, in whole or in part, into 65 languages.

The Harry Potter books have also gained recognition for sparking an interest in reading among the young at a time when children were thought to be abandoning books for computers and television, although it is reported that despite the huge uptake of the books, adolescent reading has continued to decline.

n October 1998, Warner Bros. purchased the film rights to the first two novels for a seven-figure sum. A film adaptation of Harry Potter and the Philosopher's Stone was released on 16 November 2001, and Harry Potter and the Chamber of Secrets on 15 November 2002. Both films were directed by Chris Columbus. The film version of Harry Potter and the Prisoner of Azkaban was released on 4 June 2004, directed by Alfonso Cuarón. The fourth film, Harry Potter and the Goblet of Fire, was directed by Mike Newell, and released on 18 November 2005. The film of Harry Potter and the Order of the Phoenix was released on 11 July 2007. David Yates directed, and Michael Goldenberg wrote the screenplay, having taken over the position from Steve Kloves. Harry Potter and the Half-Blood Prince was released on 15 July 2009. David Yates directed again, and Kloves returned to write the script. Warner Bros. filmed the final instalment of the series, Harry Potter and the Deathly Hallows, in two segments, with part one being released on 19 November 2010 and part two being released on 15 July 2011. Yates directed both films.

Warner Bros took considerable notice of Rowling's desires and thoughts when drafting her contract. One of her principal stipulations was the films be shot in Britain with an all-British cast, which has been generally adhered to. Rowling also demanded that Coca-Cola, the victor in the race to tie in their products to the film series, donate US$18 million to the American charity Reading is Fundamental, as well as several community charity programs.

The first four, sixth and seventh films were scripted by Steve Kloves; Rowling assisted him in the writing process, ensuring that his scripts did not contradict future books in the series. She told Alan Rickman (Severus Snape) and Robbie Coltrane (Hagrid) certain secrets about their characters before they were revealed in the books. Daniel Radcliffe (Harry Potter) asked her if Harry died at any point in the series; Rowling answered him by saying, "You have a death scene", thereby not explicitly answering the question. Director Steven Spielberg was approached to direct the first film, but dropped out. The press has repeatedly claimed that Rowling played a role in his departure, but Rowling stated that she had no say in who directed the films and would not have vetoed Spielberg. Rowling's first choice for the director had been Monty Python member Terry Gilliam, but Warner Bros. wanted a family-friendly film and chose Columbus. Rowling had gained some creative control on the films, reviewing all the scripts as well as acting as a producer on the final two-part instalment, Deathly Hallows.

Rowling, producers David Heyman and David Barron, along with directors David Yates, Mike Newell and Alfonso Cuarón collected the Michael Balcon Award for Outstanding British Contribution to Cinema at the 2011 British Academy Film Awards in honour of the Harry Potter film franchise.

In September 2013, Warner Bros. announced an "expanded creative partnership" with Rowling, based on a planned series of films about Newt Scamander, author of Fantastic Beasts and Where to Find Them. The first film will be scripted by Rowling, and be set roughly 70 years before the events of the main series. In 2014, it was announced that the series would consist of three films.

CHAPTER 26.

Success

In 2004, Forbes named Rowling as the first person to become a U.S.-dollar billionaire by writing books, the second-richest female entertainer and the 1,062nd richest person in the world. Rowling disputed the calculations and said she had plenty of money, but was not a billionaire. The 2008 Sunday Times Rich List named Rowling the 144th richest person in Britain. In 2012, Forbes removed Rowling from their rich list, claiming that her US$160 million in charitable donations and the high tax rate in the UK meant she was no longer a billionaire. In February 2013 she was assessed as the 13th most powerful woman in the United Kingdom by Woman's Hour on BBC Radio 4.

In 2001, Rowling purchased a 19th-century estate house, Killiechassie House, on the banks of the River Tay, near Aberfeldy, in Perth and Kinross.Rowling also owns a £4.5 million Georgian house in Kensington, West London, on a street with 24-hour security.

Remarriage and family

On 26 December 2001, Rowling married Neil Michael Murray (born 30 June 1971), an anaesthetist, in a private ceremony at her home, Killiechassie House, near Aberfeldy. Their son, David Gordon Rowling Murray, was born on 24 March 2003. Shortly after Rowling began writing Harry Potter and the Half-Blood Prince, she ceased working on the novel to care for David in his early infancy.

Rowling is a friend of Sarah Brown, wife of former prime minister Gordon Brown, whom she met when they collaborated on a charitable project. When Sarah Brown's son Fraser was born in 2003, Rowling was one of the first to visit her in hospital.Rowling's youngest child, daughter Mackenzie Jean Rowling Murray, to whom she dedicated Harry Potter and the Half-Blood Prince, was born on 23 January 2005.

In October 2012, a New Yorker magazine article stated that the Rowling family lived in a seventeenth-century Edinburgh house, concealed at the front by tall conifer hedges. Prior to October 2012, Rowling lived near the author Ian Rankin, who later said she was quiet and introspective, and that she seemed in her element with children. As of June 2014, the family reside in Scotland.

In 2000, Rowling established the Volant Charitable Trust, which uses its annual budget of £5.1 million to combat poverty and social inequality. The fund also gives to organisations that aid children, one parent families, and multiple sclerosis research.

Anti-poverty and children's welfare

Rowling, once a single parent, is now president of the charity Gingerbread (originally One Parent Families), having become their first Ambassador in 2000. Rowling collaborated with Sarah Brown to write a book of children's stories to aid One Parent Families.

In 2001, the UK anti-poverty fundraiser Comic Relief asked three best-selling British authors – cookery writer and TV presenter Delia Smith, Bridget Jones creator Helen Fielding, and Rowling – to submit booklets related to their most famous works for publication. Rowling's two booklets, Fantastic Beasts and Where to Find Them and Quidditch Through the Ages, are ostensibly facsimiles of books found in the Hogwarts library. Since going on sale in March 2001, the books have raised £15.7 million for the fund. The £10.8 million they have raised outside the UK have been channelled into a newly created International Fund for Children and

Young People in Crisis. In 2002 Rowling contributed a foreword to Magic, an anthology of fiction published by Bloomsbury Publishing, helping to raise money for the National Council for One Parent Families.

In 2005, Rowling and MEP Emma Nicholson founded the Children's High Level Group (now Lumos). In January 2006, Rowling went to Bucharest to highlight the use of caged beds in mental institutions for children. To further support the CHLG, Rowling auctioned one of seven handwritten and illustrated copies of The Tales of Beedle the Bard, a series of fairy tales referred to in Harry Potter and the Deathly Hallows. The book was purchased for £1.95 million by on-line bookseller Amazon.com on 13 December 2007, becoming the most expensive modern book ever sold at auction. Rowling gave away the remaining six copies to those who have a close connection with the Harry Potter books. In 2008, Rowling agreed to publish the book with the proceeds going to Lumos.On 1 June 2010 (International Children's Day), Lumos launched an annual initiative – Light a Birthday Candle for Lumos.In November 2013, Rowling handed over all earnings from the sale of The Tales of Beedle the Bard, totalling nearly £19 million.

In July 2012, Rowling was featured at the 2012 Summer Olympics opening ceremony in London where she read a few lines from J.M. Barrie's Peter Pan as part of a tribute to Great Ormond Street Children's Hospital. An inflatable representation of Lord Voldemort and other children's literary characters accompanied her reading.

CHAPTER 27.

You have Room for Improvement-

Your Setback is a Setup for your Comeback.

Smart Thinking-Smart People are Spontaneous and Very Intuitive, They Follow Their mind and they listen to wise counsel, by surrounding themselves with wise people(The Smartest). Refrain yourself from stinking thinking by reading Books like this. How do you differentiate people? By the way they think, which is a reflection of what they say, or how they talk. What comes out of their mouth. The difference between a Smart individual and a Stupid individual, is how they think. Your thought process is highly influenced by what you expose your mind to, your senses, What you see, hear, smell, feel and taste, These develop to become your perception and views about life. If you read quality books like this one in your hands right now, you can't but be successful in life. Your Actions are influenced by your choices,

You are, What you think You are. If You have the "Can do" mindset, yes you can, if you think you can, then you can. If you think you can't then you can't. Don't let other people's negativity affect how you think and how you live. You can't rise above the level of your thought. Your thoughts are so powerful that it creates a way to make anything happen. What has not been discovered is what has not been thought about. So I dare you to think. Great works are results of deep thoughts. People that make a difference in the World, are people that have dared to think differently. Inventors, Innovators and Investors. No one in this world is born with two heads, but what differentiates all of us is how we think.

Think Productively. Let your thinking produce results and improve the quality of your life. Think ahead. Asides having a positive Mental Attitude. You must think ahead. Think of Possibilities, even when things don't work out as thought or planned. Rethink, sometimes we say think twice, but I will advice you rethink because sometimes your second thought is even worse than the first and sometimes worsens the situation. Don't be too lazy to think. Put your brain cells to work, don't allow your head be full of junk, Thoughts that are meaningless. Agitating over what can't be changed. Worrying over the system.
Smart Mind- Let me tell you a little about the smart mind. To be smart minded is Wisdom but to be empty minded is foolishness and can be very costly. We talked about being smart or being stupid.

Smart Ideas-

Change your game plan, Re strategize if you have to, Open your mind. Ideas are like rain, and it can come unannounced. You don't need a retentive memory to be smart. Smart people keep their notepads around, all the time. This makes them write or type on their notepad.
Social Media Frenzy- Don't be caught up in the Social Media Frenzy, Wasting time on profane tweets and vain pictures. You add Thousands and even Millions of Friends and followers on daily bases, yet you have

nothing to show for it. Some Countries in the World have less population than your followers and friends. My question to you is Have you not heard of Network Marketing? How you can use the advantage of numbers to expand and grow.

Work Smart- The Hardest Worker is not the highest paid, but the smartest worker. You boss needs result and your work strategy doesn't really matter to him. There's no excuse for failure. Complaining will never solve a thing. Always think of the way forward. People don't really care how much you know. Infact knowing too much sometimes can be annoying, because it gives no room for productive thinking.

Always take steps in the right direction. Quit bad habits hindering you from moving forward. Habits develop over time till it becomes a character. Smart choice is, develop good habits and let it form your character. Don't be too sluggish, giving excuses over everything. Speak up when neccessary.

You can't sit around crying over spilled milk, you have to move on. Life is not a bed of roses. What you sow, you reap. If you want better life, you have to create one. People buy your personality before they buy what you selling, The way you present yourself says a lot about who you are. People's view about you, starts from your appearance before you say anything. Your dressing determines how you are addressed. You are addressed the way you dress. You don't have to be a fashionista to wear good clothes and dress well. Look Smart, Neat and Stay Clean. Your self-confidence is complete in your appearance. Never leave home looking untidy. People's confidence in you is determined first on the way you present yourself. Your self presentation determines how well you sell yourself. If are given a odd look, on your appearance, the first thing you want to check is your dress. Develop an excellent dress sense. Look good, because Good looks is Good Business. Smart people always look smart. Watch what you eat, eat healthy, sleep well and work-out. Smart people are always prepared for opportunities that come their way. The end they say *justifies the means. Nothing in this World happens by chance, be always ready for change, because change is the only constant thing in life. Your Work plan on daily bases should be work in progress, even when you achieve your goals, Set new ones. Create a Standard for your life. Never settle for the ordinary. Go for more, never relax on the norms, strive for the next level.*

Smart Choice-No matter what life throws at you, you have the choice to accept it or reject it. It may take sometime, but your choice will prevail in the end. Oftentimes we are victims of our own choice, but we have the will power to reverse that choice and come back better. Our lives reflects our choices either good or bad. We are proofs of our own choices. No one is responsible for the way we live our lives. No one can live your life for you. You choices are a results of how your life turns out.
Experience they say is the best teacher True , but it doesn't have to be your own experience. You can learn from other people's experiences. That's what smart people do. Smart people use other people's experience to do better.

CHAPTER 28.

Smart Action-

Don't just be an Individual that knows it all. People that know it all don't go far in life. They are often stagnant. They ain't going nowhere, you know why? Just because they are not taking action. Don't be a jack of all trades, master of none.

Take deliberate steps on what you know. Step out in Faith, Make decisive actions, be very clear in your mind and don't be confused. It's not just about what you know, but what you do with it. What are you doing with what you know? Don't let your brain be another shelf of so many great books wasting away. Do something with what you know. Let what you know improve your life for the best.

Smart Relationships-

Everybody can't be your friend, so stop trying to impress everybody. The best people in the World have very few quality friends. Keep healthy relationships and nurture it. It's called Smart Relationship. People that add value to your life. People that want to see you grow and succeed. People that encourage you to do better. People that positively criticize you. People that tell you the truth, even when you don't like it. A lot of people can deceive you, and you won't even know it. Most times people that know you are the ones that pull you down the most and don't want you to do better than them because your success is a threat to them. They are simply jealous and envious. They covet you in a bad way. They always wish it was them. They want to take your place or even replace you at all cost and by all means. Your worst enemies are very close to you, that's if you ain't your own worst enemy, it's called enemy from within.

Smart Timing-

Time is everything. Do the right thing at the Right Time. Time is Money, meaning the value of time precious. You can lose money and make it back, but time can't. Time waits for no one. Be Smart in your time schedule and To-Do-list. Your life time-table starts the day you were born and ends when you die. Whatever you do in your onetime lifetime is what you filled in it. What do you do with your time and how do you spend your time. Life is short. Be proactive and Make the best use of your time, what you spend your time doing, is the reward you get from life. If you spend your quality time doing something, worthwhile, you will gain the result. Don't waste time, it's of great value. If you value time, Money will be your servant. You trade your time for money.

Sometime, people don't really pay for what you know, they pay for your time. Never procrastinate. Do it now, if you fail to do the right thing at the right time, you will struggle to get it done, if you ever get it done. Life is programmed to be progressive, if you waste time, you will be left behind and probably forgotten. Somethings became outdated because, the time is over. Be apt and accurate. You don't have to be perfect, but be accurate and live with excellence. Plan your time wisely and do what you have to do. Don't rush into doing things, but be timely in your deeds.
What ever it is that takes most of your resources like money, time and energy on daily bases, can be a pointer to where you need to invest your money or start your own business.

Better still you will have people around that will give you all the support you need and reference you for what you need.
Make Your Money Work for You-Don't ever work for Money, make your money work for you. Use your money as a tool to open doors of opportunity. Go to places where the rich hang out. Attend events they attend. Talk big if you ever get an opportunity to speak at a meeting. Position yourself in a rich perspective. Give people a rich impression.

Always act like a rqRich Person. No one knows, how much you have in your bank account anyway or your net worth.

Think Smart-

Always talk about solutions, ideas, better ways of doing things. Don't backbite or slander people. It gives a negative impression of you. If you must criticize, criticize constructively. If you must give your opinion, never give negative opinions. Be positive at all times and always talk positively. Develop a positive mindset and think positively.

Give people the impression that you are around to help and add value to their life, even when they don't offer you anything in return.
Let your personality attract the people to you, Call the shots by creating the opportunity, with your excellent words of solution then you can name your price. Give true life experiences of your past achievements and milestones. Share stories about your strengths and your abilities. It creates room for opportunities. Never you talk about your weaknesses and don't ever talk about your past failures. Its repulsive.
People believe more in you when you always talk about possibilities.
People trust you more when you always talk about your positive lifestyle.
Let me then, tell you the difference between Arrogance, Pride and Attitude.

CHAPTER 29.

Financial. Independence.
Success, Business and Financial Principles are no respecter of your color, gender, age, race or location.
Wealth and Asset Management- Every Cent Matters. Let me tell you a secret, you will be shocked to know that the wealth of the rich is accumulated or en-massed from billions of cents. Some billion dollar businesses only make less than $1 profit which is 99cent and below for each product. Becoming a billionaire doesn't start from billions, it starts from cents. Droplets of water are what makes a mighty ocean. Multiples of trees make a mighty forest. A single tree can never make a mighty forest. Start small but see the big goal.
Finally, after all this smart talk...my question to you is, what can you give in exchange for your soul? Absolutely nothing. Prosperity is a matter of the soul. Don't sell it.

Smart Ideas-I shared some of my Money Smart Ideas with a friend and she said, the market for that business is already about a competitive market. Then as a Mentor I told her that, I have given you a clue, it's now your responsibility to go and search for ideas, that will make you stand out in that market, carve your niche. A word is enough for the wise. I went further to tell her that. Even if it's a fresh idea and no one has ever done it before, do you think other people won't start and compete with you? There's something that will always make you outstanding and different to distinguish you in whatever you put your heart to do. Search for it, Discover it and Display it. That is, your Gold Myne.
Wealth Management- Every cent matters, don't ever underestimate the loose change. Imagine you make a profit margin of one cent or one dollar on 100 million items?

Smart Mind-

Develop a Smart Mind it's a Gold Mine. Your mind is the battlefield of your life, where you win or lose the challenges of life in the reality. Your thought process is a key factor when it comes to developing a Smart Mind. A positive mental attitude is a great asset.

Work Smart-

Intelligence is a Result of Diligence. Stop The Hard Work and Start working Smart, That's Diligence. I said earlier, that the Hardest worker is never the highest paid anywhere in the world in any organization in life. Multiple Streams Of Income-Don't ever Settle for Average or less. I want you to know that the Rich Invest in Businesses, or set up a business for the middle class and low income earners to...then control the market and sometimes determine your spending power through demand and supply.

Work Smart- What is your earning power? How much do you make? What is your income, your revenue and your cash flow.
The Work Smart- Are the Skilled, the Innovators, They are great salespeople.
The hardest Workers are never the highest paid, but the smartest workers are because they produce better results. Don't just work hard. Work Smart. It's not about how far you go in life, but how well you do.

The Truth in This Smart Book is one of the World best kept Secrets that are Never Taught or Learnt in the Worlds best Ivy League Schools.
Smart Time- Reminisce a minute on what takes most of your time on daily bases. If whatever it is doesn't add any value to your life or its worth the while, then Quit.

Where your treasure is, there will your heart be, meaning what you think about most in life takes most of your time. It may not really be your work or your investment or money.

You will need to change your mindset. If you happen to be a housewife and you take care of the home and kids. That may be a good idea to start a daycare or a kiddies playground in the neighborhood or the community.

Be Money Wise-
Money Wise is not about how you spend, but how you make money. Wisdom is the Principal of Money. Without wisdom you can never be rich. If you get rich by chance, you can't stay rich. You need Wisdom to get rich and Stay rich.

CHAPTER 30.

Money Smart-
You don't dilly dally on your decisions when it comes to money. You have to be very objective and single minded. You can't be double minded. Take time to think through it thoroughly. Your thought process should be at its peak. Some Financial Opportunities are seasonal and some come with time. Either way. You have to be Money Smart. Invest in the right ventures. I am sure you know of people who use to be very rich sometime ago, but are. now dead broke. You don't want that to be your story. If you by any chance fall into this category, then this is the time to move on. This is the time to let go. Pick your life up again and move on. You must have learnt your lessons and become smarter. You must know that it's not that Smart people don't make mistakes. No one Is above mistakes. But the difference is, smart people have learnt to manage their mistakes, that in the end, it all looks like a smart mistake, because it turns out in their favor because they have the mind set of all things work together for good.

Right now, I know a lot of people are in a deep financial mess. Don't worry about it. The good news is, stop any activity or habits that keep you perpetually broke. Insanity they say, is doing the same thing, same way and expecting a different result. It may be a foolish financial decision or investment in your own case. Don't worry, you can bounce back. Now you know where you went wrong. Explore other financial opportunities available around you every day and tap into it. In some other cases, it's something you spend on from time to time or something you pay for consistently, that you don't really need. Cut cost to the barest minimum. You don't have to pay for what you can do yourself or what you can get without having to pay for. Rome they say was not built in a day. Same way the Earth was not created in a day. Don't join the bandwagon of the get rich quick or overnight millionaires.

Anything you don't value will be lost. Sustaining great wealth takes time. According to the law of gravity, we know that whatever goes up, must come down. But the law of Growth states that whatever grows up stays up. Great Riches only obey the law of multiplication. A situation where you invest in profitable ventures.

Simply because you are making so much money today, doesn't mean, you will be making so much money tomorrow. Remember the parable of the rich fool? Today is guaranteed tomorrow is not. Make the best use of your financial opportunity today. Opportunity comes but once, when it's lost it may never return. That's why you see some people who were once rich, then got broke and they never recovered ever again. With time comes opportunities with opportunities comes responsibilities. If you use it wisely, then you smart. A word is enough for the wise. The difference between the Money Smart and others is that the smart money invest their resources in any opportunity that will multiply their wealth and grow their riches. Money, Time, Energy and other resources. It's not only money that makes you rich, but your net worth. and your network determines your Net worth.

No amount is too small to invest in a profitable venture. Calculate the amount of money you spend on different things on daily basis, then monthly, then annually. You will realize that if you had invested that money, you would have made twice as much as you have now. How much do you earn, what's your income? How much do you spend? What are your expenses on daily bases, monthly and annually. Some expenses are inevitable, like food, rent, bills and fees. You may want to invest in this area too. Let me give you an idea. This is my personal experience and it's been working for me for over a decade. I invest my money in the areas I spend most. That way I become a player in that trade e.g real estate, food and beverage business and distribution, clothing line and fashion, leisure and entertainment. If you look into these areas very well, you will discover that it's hard for anyone to do without those needs.

Invest your money in areas of human needs, things people can never do without. That way you will always be in business. In and out of season.

Let's talk about trade a little bit- Business is all about trade, either you are selling a product or offering a service. You get paid in the process and that's how you make profit. If you are paying less than you deserve or less than the quality of your service and product then you losing. Same thing about your job. You are simply trading your time for money. Therefore if you are paid less than the quality of the time you put in, then you are losing. Sometimes we can invest our time for a lifetime achievement or reward. This takes time, when you have to invest your resources in a long-term project. You need to be very patient and be hopeful and optimistic. That's like a farmer who sows during seed time and will expect to harvest during harvest time. If you invest your resources in a long-term financial project, you can't expect the prospect overnight or as soon as possible.

You need to give time for the gestation period. You need to take time to nurture your investment and watch it grow. Let me cite an illustration. If a farmer sows or plants, seeds during seed time and he decides to harvest before harvest time. Then he has defeated the purpose of seed time and harvest time, therefore he will lose the seed and the harvest just because he hears so impatient. The same example goes for an expectant mother, who is pregnant but can't wait for 9 months. What happens, she will give birth to a premature baby, which is unhealthy and post threat to the life of the baby. It may take days, months and sometimes years to gain Return On Investment known as ROI. What you shouldn't fail to do is not to invest as often as possible. Invest in different areas of investment opportunities.

Use your abilities to add value to your life, profit with your talent and gifts. That's God's natural investment in you. You don't have to be educated to discover your talent and the gift. What you have but you don't use will soon be useless and will be wasted. Remember the parable of the Talents. Its time you discover, develop and display your talent.

Develop yourself, build your abilities and Train your skills, then always practice. The highest paid athletes and entertainers practice always, not because they are necessarily better than their colleagues, but they are Smart enough to practice always.

They stick to their routine and discipline enough to follow their daily To-Do-List. Its not rocket science, no amount of technology can change the principles of Financial Freedom and Prosperity. If you are are money smart, you will always smile to the bank but If you are not, you will always frown at your bank statement. Its Time you set some money aside from your earnings as saving. Let me tell you how. You can save at least $1 a day.   By month end you would have saved $30. Some people can save $2 a day some $5 some $10 or more depending on how convenient it is foe you to save. Not depending on how much you make, but how convenient it is for you. This saving can be used as Emergency Savings, You can pay an emergency bill, and you can also invest the money on trade, buying and selling or any profitable business venture. No amount is too small to invest. Lets use my $1 a day savings principle as a case study. $1/Day. Anybody can do it. Because $1 can be easily saved. Its not as easy as it sounds if you are not committed and disciplined to stay focus. If you save $1/day then you have $30/Month and $360/Annum. If you can save $2/day then you have $60/Month and $720/Annum. If you can save $5/day then you have $150/Month and $1800/Annum. If yours is $10/day, you have $300/Month and $3600/Annum. This savings can then be used to start any business you desire. You can then Get Rich Smart.

This brings us to our next Topic.

CHAPTER 31.

Financial Goal Setting.

We all celebrate the New Year with Joy and Excitement but forget to set our financial goals. No nation on earth, will start the year without their fiscal goals, their budget and the money market. So why can't we as individuals or family do the same thing or even better. Companies and Corporations Set their Financial Goals and clearly set their Annual Revenues and Expenditures. You can be surprised that the M.D/CEO or even the company CFO (Chief Financial Officer) has no personal financial goals for the year. Its not rocket science and like I said, you don't have to be educated to be Money Smart. Remember the story I shared earlier about my illiterate Grandma?

Stay focused on your goals and set a desired result for yourself. Have a standard for your life. Your Age has got nothing to do with it. I joke with my friends that make money, when you can enjoy it. Because time is of essence.
Nuture a Smart Relationship and sometimes it's not all about what's in for you or what you stand to gain, but about trust, confidence and your credibility. When you need favors you will have someone to call.

The Good News is that-This Smart Book Guarantee's you a Better Chance of Getting Rich and as often as you read this book, you have a chance of getting Richer only if you take action on what you learn from it.
Anyone can be rich at anytime. But not everyone can be rich everytime, meaning not everyone can Stay Rich!. Anyone can become successful at anytime but not everyone can Remain Successful. That's where this book comes in, and it will be very important in your life. This Smart book will help you develop Financial prudence, will teach you Financial intelligence, How you can Maintain Your Riches, and pass it on to your next Generation,

How you can build a Wealth Legacy and a Prosperous Empire, You will Know everything about Finanncial Freedom or Liberty and be Armed Passion with Financial Knowledge. If you succeed or fail, you take the credit or the blame. No one will. Success has many fathers but failure is a Bastard. No one will ever want to identify with failure. Dare to Succeed. Revenge your haters and enemies with your success.

FINANCING YOUR IDEA-

-Better still you will have people around that will give you all the support you need and reference you for what you need.
Make Your Money Work for You-Don't ever work for Money, make your money work for you. Use your money as a tool to open doors of opportunity. Go to places where the rich hang out. Attend events they attend. Talk big if you ever get an opportunity to speak at a meeting. Position yourself in a rich perspective. Give people a rich impression. Always act like a rqRich Person. No one knows, how much you have in your bank account anyway or your net worth.

Think Smart- Always talk about solutions, ideas, better ways of doing things. Don't backbite or slander people. It gives a negative impression of you. If you must criticize, criticize constructively. If you must give your opinion, never give negative opinions. Be positive at all times and always talk positive. Develop a positive mindset and think positively.
Give the rich the impression that you are around to help them make more money and add value to their business even when they don't offer you anything in return.

Let your personality attract the rich to you, Call the shorts by creating the opportunity, with your excellent words of solution then you can name your price.

Share true life experiences of your past achievements and milestones. Share stories about your strengths and your abilities. It creates room for opportunities. Never you talk about your weaknesses and don't ever talk about your past failures. Its repulsive.

People believe more in you when you always talk about possibilities.
People trust you more when you always talk about your positive lifestyle.
Let me then, tell you the difference between Arrogance, Pride and Attitude.

Financial. Independence.

Success, Business and Financial Principles is no respecter of your color, gender, age, race or location.

Wealth and Asset Management- Every Cent Matters. Let me tell you a secret, you will be shocked to know that the wealth of the rich is accumulated or enmassed from billions of cents. Some billion dollar businesses only make less than $1 profit which is 99cent and below on each product. Becoming a billionaire doesn't start from billions, it starts from cents. Droplets of water is what makes a mighty ocean. Multiples of trees makes a mighty forest. A single tree can never make a mighty forest. Start small but see the big goal.

Finally, after all this smart talk...my question to you is, what can you give in exchange for your soul? Absolutely nothing. Prosperity is a matter of the soul. Don't sell it.

I shared some of my Money Smart Ideas with a friend and she said, the market for that business is already saturated with lots of competitors, then I told her that, I have given her a clue, it's then her responsibility to go and search for ideas, that will make her stand out in the market place, carve your niche. A word is enough for the wise. I went further to tell her that. Even if it's a fresh idea and no one has ever done it before, do you think other people won't start and compete with you? There's something that will always make you different and distinguished. Search for it, Discover it and Display it. That is your Gold Myne.

Wealth Management- Every cent matters, don't ever
Smart Mind- Develop a Smart Mind it's a Gold Mine. Your mind is the battle field of your life, where you win or lose the challenges of life in the reality. Your thought process is a key factor when it comes to developing a Smart Mind. A positive mental attitude is a great asset.

Work Smart- Financing your idea.

Multiple Streams Of Income-Don't ever Settle for Average or less. I want you to know that the Rich Invest in Businesses, or set up business for the middle class and low income earners to...then control the market and sometimes determine your spending power through demand and supply.

Work Smart- Better still you will have people around that will give you all the support you need and reference you for what you need.
Make Your Money Work for You-Don't ever work for Money, make your money work for you. Use your money as a tool to open doors of opportunity. Go to places where the rich hang out. Attend events they attend. Talk big if you ever get an opportunity to speak at a meeting. Position yourself in a rich perspective. Give people a rich impression. Always act like a rqRich Person. No one knows, how much you have in your bank account anyway or your net worth.

CHAPTER 32.

Think Smart- Always talk about solutions, ideas, better ways of doing things. Don't backbite or slander people. It gives a negative impression of you. If you must criticize, criticize constructively. If you must give your opinion, never give negative opinions. Be positive at all times and always talk positive. Develop a positive mindset and think positively.

Give the rich the impression that you are around to help them make more money and add value to their business even when they don't offer you anything in return.

Smart Ideas-I shared some of my Money Smart Ideas with a friend and she said, the market for that business is already about a competitive market. Then as a Mentor I told her that, I have given you a clue, it's now your responsibility to go and search for ideas, that will make you stand out in that market, carve your niche. A word is enough for the wise. I went further to tell her that. Even if it's a fresh idea and no one has ever done it before, do you think other people won't start and compete with you? There's something that will always make you different and distinguished. Search for it, Discover it and Display it. That is your Gold Mine.

Wealth Management- Every cent matters, don't ever look down on or down grade the piggy bank.

Smart Mind- Develop a Smart Mind it's a Gold Mine. Your mind is the battlefield of your life, where you win or lose the challenges of life in the reality. Your thought process is a key factor when it comes to developing a Smart Mind. A positive mental attitude is a great asset.

Work Smart-Multiple Streams Of Income-Don't ever Settle for Average or less. I want you to know that the Rich Invest in Businesses, or set up a business for the middle class and low income earners to...then control the market and sometimes determine your spending power through demand and supply.

Work Smart- What is your earning power? How much do you make? What is your income, your revenue and your cash flow.

Book Smart- The Insight and Secrets hidden in this book, are what the rich don't want you to ever know. The rich hide their success secrets from others (The middle-class and the poor) by putting it in a book. Develop the habit of reading. It's a Gold Mine. The Worlds best kept secrets and Great treasures are not hidden anywhere else except in books.

Work Smart- If You are going through a Stress in any area of your life, especially in your Work or relationships Note that Wisdom is Lacking. Crave for wisdom, The best I can do is to motivate you to get wisdom and teach you how to manage your stress, and the best and easiest way to manage your stress is to stop worrying, stop complaining, stop making excuses and stop Mormoring. Get up and do something about your situation or just simply ignore it. Wisdom is doing something about what can be changed, doing nothing about what can't be changed and the ability and wisdom to know the difference.

Financial Principles respect, no age, Gender, Color, race, time or location, the principles are universal. Success can happen anywhere in the World.

Financing Your Idea-A wiseman once said, if You have nothing to offer, no One gives You Recognition

The rich and Money Smart don't Do Business on credit. They Do Business on Merit, Integrity and Trust because our Word is our Bond because Trust and sincerity is the sole of business. Put your Trust to the Test, be a

Person of your words, let people take You for your words. Somestimes You may have to put something at Stake as collateral. Thats where the issue of loan comes in.

When Trust is abused Then You need to sacrifice what You have that's worth much more than the money You Need. Don't ever enter a business deal or going into any venture without clear definition of the terms and rules of engagement. Don't do business without stating in clear terms the agreement. Get it right and do your paper works correctly. Don't ever ignore documents. Never give your consent or sign any contract if you are not satisfied with the terms. Remember, we talked about the books, keep your books right and seek the help and assistance of experts, consultants and advisors in the area you intend venturing into.

CHAPTER 33

Winfrey was named "Orpah" after the biblical character in the Book of Ruth on her birth certificate, but people mispronounced it regularly and Oprah stuck. Winfrey was born in Kosciusko, Mississippi, to an unmarried teenage mother. She later said that her conception was due to a single sexual encounter and the couple broke up not long after. Her mother, Vernita Lee (born 1935), was a housemaid. Winfrey had believed that her biological father was Vernon Winfrey (born 1933), a coal miner turned barber turned city councilman who had been in the Armed Forces when she was born. Decades later, Mississippi farmer and World War II veteran Noah Robinson, Sr. (born c. 1925) claimed to be her biological father. A genetic test in 2006 determined that her matrilineal line originated among the Kpelle ethnic group, in the area that today is Liberia. Her genetic makeup was determined to be 89% Sub-Saharan African, 8% Native American, and 3% East Asian. However, the East Asian may, given the imprecisions of genetic testing, actually be Native American markers.

After Winfrey's birth, her mother traveled north and Winfrey spent her first six years living in rural poverty with her maternal grandmother, Hattie Mae (Presley)

Lee (April 15, 1900 – February 27, 1963), who was so poor that Winfrey often wore dresses made of potato sacks, for which the local children made fun of her.

Her grandmother taught her to read before the age of three and took her to the local church, where she was nicknamed "The Preacher" for her ability to recite Bible verses. When Winfrey was a child, her grandmother would hit her with a stick when she did not do chores or if she misbehaved in any way.

At age six, Winfrey moved to an inner-city neighborhood in Milwaukee, Wisconsin with her mother Vernita Lee, who was less supportive and encouraging than her grandmother had been, largely as a result of the long hours she worked as a maid. Around this time, Lee had given birth to another daughter, Winfrey's younger half-sister, Patricia who later (in February 2003, at age 43) died of causes related to cocaine addiction. By 1962, Lee was having difficulty raising both daughters so Winfrey was temporarily sent to live with Vernon in Nashville, Tennessee. While Winfrey was in Nashville, Lee gave birth to a third daughter who was put up for adoption (in the hope of easing the financial straits that had led to Lee's being on welfare) and later also named Patricia. Winfrey did not learn she had a second half-sister until 2010. By the time Winfrey moved back in with Lee, Lee had also given birth to a boy named Jeffrey, Winfrey's half-brother, who died of AIDS-related causes in 1989.

Winfrey has stated she was molested by her cousin, uncle, and a family friend, starting when she was nine years old, something she first announced to her viewers on a 1986 episode of her TV show regarding sexual abuse.

When Winfrey discussed the alleged abuse with family members at age 24, they refused to accept what she said. Winfrey once commented that she had chosen not to be a mother because she had not been mothered well.

At 13, after suffering years of abuse, Winfrey ran away from home. When she was 14, she became pregnant but her son died shortly after birth. She later stated she felt betrayed by the family member who had sold the story to the National Enquirer in 1990. She began going to Lincoln High School; but after early success in the Upward Bound program, was transferred to the affluent suburban Nicolet High School, where she says her poverty was constantly rubbed in her face as she rode the bus to school with fellow African-Americans, some of whom were servants of her classmates' families. She began to steal money from her mother in an effort to keep up with her free-spending peers, to lie to and argue with her mother, and to go out with older boys.

Her frustrated mother once again sent her to live with Vernon in Nashville, Tennessee, though this time she did not take her back. Vernon was strict, but encouraging, and made her education a priority. Winfrey became an honors student, was voted Most Popular Girl, and joined her high school speech team at

East Nashville High School, placing second in the nation in dramatic interpretation.

She won an oratory contest, which secured her a full scholarship to Tennessee State University, a historically black institution, where she studied communication. Her first job as a teenager was working at a local grocery store. At age 17, Winfrey won the Miss Black Tennessee beauty pageant.[46] She also attracted the attention of the local black radio station, WVOL, which hired her to do the news part-time. She worked there during her senior year of high school, and again while in her first two years of college.

Winfrey's career choice in media would not have surprised her grandmother, who once said that ever since Winfrey could talk, she was on stage. As a child, she played games interviewing her corncob doll and the crows on the fence of her family's property. Winfrey later acknowledged her grandmother's influence, saying it was Hattie Mae who had encouraged her to speak in public and "gave me a positive sense of myself". Working in local media, she was both the youngest news anchor and the first black female news anchor at Nashville's WLAC-TV. She moved to Baltimore's WJZ-TV in 1976 to co-anchor the six o'clock news. She was then recruited to join Richard Sher as co-host of WJZ's local talk show People Are Talking, which premiered on August 14, 1978. She also hosted the local version of

Dialing for Dollars there.

Born in rural poverty, then raised by a mother on welfare in a poor urban neighborhood, Winfrey became a millionaire at age 32 when her talk show went national. Winfrey was in a position to negotiate ownership of the show and start her own production company because of the success and the amount of revenue the show generated. At age 41, Winfrey had a net worth of $340 million and replaced Bill Cosby as the only African American on the Forbes 400. With a 2000 net worth of $800 million, Winfrey is believed to be the richest African American of the 20th century. Owing to her status as a historical figure, Professor Juliet E.K. Walker of the University of Illinois created the course "History 298: Oprah Winfrey, the Tycoon." Winfrey was the highest paid TV entertainer in the United States in 2006, earning an estimated $260 million during the year, five times the sum earned by second-place music executive Simon Cowell. By 2008, her yearly income had increased to $275 million.

Forbes' international rich list has listed Winfrey as the world's only black billionaire from 2004 to 2006 and as the first black woman billionaire in world history. As of 2014 Winfrey has a net worth in excess of 2.9 billion dollars and has overtaken former eBay CEO Meg Whitman as the richest self-made woman in America.

CHAPTER 34.

Winfrey at the White House for the 2010 Kennedy Center Honors

Winfrey was called "arguably the world's most powerful woman" by CNN and

Time.com, "arguably the most influential woman in the world" by The American

Spectator, "one of the 100 people who most influenced the 20th Century" and "one

of the most influential people" from 2004 to 2011 by TIME. Winfrey is the only

person in the world to have appeared in the latter list on all eight occasions.

At the end of the 20th century Life listed Winfrey as both the most influential

woman and the most influential black person of her generation, and in a cover-

story profile the magazine called her "America's most powerful woman". In 2007,

USA Today ranked Winfrey as the most influential woman and most influential

black person of the previous quarter-century. Ladies Home Journal also ranked

Winfrey number one in their list of the most powerful women in America and

senator Barack Obama has said she "may be the most influential woman in the

country". In 1998 Winfrey became the first woman and first African American to

top Entertainment Weekly's list of the 101 most powerful people in the

entertainment industry. Forbes named her the world's most powerful celebrity in

2005, 2007, 2008, 2010 and 2013. She has also been listed as one of the most powerful 100 women in the world by Forbes, ranking fourteenth in 2014.

In 2010, Life magazine named Winfrey one of the 100 people who changed the world, alongside such luminaries as Jesus Christ, Elvis Presley and Lady Mary Wortley Montagu. Winfrey was the only living woman to make the list.

Columnist Maureen Dowd seems to agree with such assessments: "She is the top alpha female in this country. She has more credibility than the president. Other successful women, such as Hillary Clinton and Martha Stewart, had to be publicly slapped down before they could move forward. Even Condi has had to play the protegé with Bush. None of this happened to Oprah – she is a straight ahead success story. Vanity Fair wrote: "Oprah Winfrey arguably has more influence on the culture than any university president, politician, or religious leader, except perhaps the Pope. Bill O'Reilly said: "this is a woman that came from nothing to rise up to be the most powerful woman, I think, in the world. I think Oprah Winfrey is the most powerful woman in the world, not just in America. That's – anybody who goes on her program immediately benefits through the roof. I mean, she has a loyal following; she has credibility; she has talent; and she's done it on her own to become fabulously wealthy and fabulously powerful."

In 2005, Winfrey was named the greatest woman in American history as part of a public poll as part of The Greatest American. She was ranked No. 9 overall on the list of greatest Americans. However polls estimating Winfrey's personal popularity have been inconsistent.

A November 2003 Gallup poll estimated that 73% of American adults had a favorable view of Winfrey. Another Gallup poll in January 2007 estimated the figure at 74%, although it dropped to 66% when Gallup conducted the same poll in October 2007. A December 2007 Fox News poll put the figure at 55%. According to Gallup's annual most admired poll, Americans consistently rank Winfrey as one of the most admired women in the world. Her highest rating came in 2007, when she was statistically tied with Hillary Clinton for first place. In a list compiled by the British magazine New Statesman in September 2010, she was voted 38th in the list of "The World's 50 Most Influential Figures 2010".

"Oprahfication"

The Wall Street Journal coined the term "Oprahfication", meaning public confession as a form of therapy. By confessing intimate details about her weight problems, tumultuous love life, and sexual abuse, and crying alongside her guests, Time magazine credits Winfrey with creating a new form of media communication known as "rapport talk" as distinguished from the "report talk" of Phil Donahue: "Winfrey saw television's power to blend public and private; while it links strangers and conveys information over public airwaves, TV is most often viewed in the privacy of our homes. Like a family member, it sits down to meals with us and talks to us in the lonely afternoons. Grasping this paradox, .She makes people care because she cares.

That is Winfrey's genius, and will be her legacy, as the changes she has wrought in the talk show continue to permeate our culture and shape our lives."

Observers have also noted the "Oprahfication" of politics such as "Oprah-style debates" and Bill Clinton being described as "the man who brought Oprah-style psychobabble and misty confessions to politics."Newsweek stated: "Every time a politician lets his lip quiver or a cable anchor 'emotes' on TV, they nod to the cult of confession that Oprah helped create. Winfrey's disclosures about her weight (which peaked at 108 kg (238 lb)) also paved the way for other plus-sized women in media[citation needed] such as Roseanne Barr, Rosie O'Donnell and Star Jones. The November 1988 Ms. observed that "in a society where fat is taboo, she made it in a medium that worships thin and celebrates a bland, white-bread prettiness of body and personality. But Winfrey made fat sexy, elegant – damned near gorgeous – with her drop-dead wardrobe, easy body language, and cheerful sensuality."

CHAPTER 35.

"The Oprah Effect"

*The power of Winfrey's opinions and endorsement to influence public opinion,
especially consumer purchasing choices, has been dubbed "The Oprah Effect".
The effect has been documented or alleged in domains as diverse as book sales,
beef markets, and election voting. Late in 1996, Winfrey introduced the Oprah's
Book Club segment to her television show. The segment focused on new books
and classics and often brought obscure novels to popular attention. The book club
became such a powerful force that whenever Winfrey introduced a new book as
her book-club selection, it instantly became a best-seller; for example, when she
selected the classic John Steinbeck novel East of Eden, it soared to the top of the
book charts. Being recognized by Winfrey often means a million additional book
sales for an author. In Reading with Oprah: The Book Club that Changed America
(2005), Kathleen Rooney describes Winfrey as "a serious American intellectual*

who pioneered the use of electronic media, specifically television and the Internet, to take reading – a decidedly non-technological and highly individual act – and highlight its social elements and uses in such a way to motivate millions of erstwhile non-readers to pick up books."

When author Jonathan Franzen's book was selected for the Book Club, he reportedly "cringed" and said selected books tend to be "schmaltzy".

After James Frey's A Million Little Pieces was found to contain fabrications in 2006, Winfrey confronted him on her show over the breach of trust. In 2009, Winfrey apologized to Frey for the public confrontation. During a show about mad cow disease with Howard Lyman (aired on April 16, 1996), Winfrey said she was stopped cold from eating another burger. Texas cattlemen sued her and Lyman in early 1998 for "false defamation of perishable food" and "business disparagement", claiming that Winfrey's remarks sent cattle prices tumbling, costing beef producers $11 million. Winfrey was represented by attorney Chip Babcock and, on February 26, after a two-month trial in an Amarillo, Texas court, a jury found Winfrey and Lyman were not liable for damages. During the lawsuit, Winfrey hired Phil McGraw's company Courtroom Sciences, Inc. to help her analyze and read the jury. McGraw made such an impression on Winfrey that she invited him to appear on her show. He accepted the invitation and appeared regularly on The Oprah Winfrey Show before launching his own show, Dr. Phil, created in 2002 by Winfrey's production company, Harpo Productions, in partnership with CBS Paramount, which produced the show.[citation needed] Winfrey's ability to launch other successful talk shows such as Dr. Phil, Dr. Oz and Rachael Ray has also been cited as examples of "The Oprah Effect".

Winfrey joins Barack and Michelle Obama on the campaign trail (December 10, 2007).

Winfrey endorsed presidential candidate Barack Obama in the 2008 presidential election, the first time she endorsed a political candidate running for office. Winfrey held a fundraiser for Obama on September 8, 2007, at her Santa Barbara estate. In December 2007, Winfrey joined Obama for a series of rallies in the early primary states of Iowa, New Hampshire, and South Carolina. The Columbia, South Carolina event on December 9, 2007, drew a crowd of nearly 30,000, the largest for any political event of 2007. An analysis by two economists at the University of Maryland, College Park estimated that Winfrey's endorsement was responsible for between 420,000 and 1,600,000 votes for Obama in the Democratic primary alone, based on a sample of states that did not include Texas, Michigan, North Dakota, Kansas, or Alaska. The results suggest that in the sampled states, Winfrey's endorsement was responsible for the difference in the popular vote between Barack Obama and Hillary Clinton. The governor of Illinois, Rod Blagojevich, reported being so impressed by Winfrey's endorsement that he considered offering Winfrey Obama's vacant senate seat describing Winfrey as "the most instrumental person in electing Barack Obama president", with "a voice larger than all 100 senators combined". Winfrey responded by stating that although she was absolutely not interested, she did feel she could be a senator.

In April 2014, Winfrey spoke for more than 20 minutes at a fundraiser in Arlington, Virginia, for Lavern Chatman, a candidate in a primary to nominate a Democratic Party candidate for election to the U.S. House of Representatives. Winfrey participated in the event even after reports had revealed that Chatman had been found liable in 2001 for her role in a scheme to defraud hundreds of District of Columbia nursing home employees of at least $1.4 million in owed wages.

The viewership for The Oprah Winfrey Show was highest during the 1991–92 season, when about 13.1 million U.S. viewers were watching each day. By 2003, ratings declined to 7.4 million daily viewers. Ratings briefly rebounded to approximately 9 million in 2005 and then declined again to around 7.3 million viewers in 2008, though it remained the highest rated talk show. In 2008, Winfrey's show was airing in 140 countries internationally and seen by an estimated 46 million people in the US weekly. According to the Harris poll, Winfrey was America's favorite television personality in 1998, 2000, 2002–06, and 2009. Winfrey was especially popular among women, Democrats, political moderates,

Baby Boomers, Generation X, Southern Americans and East Coast Americans. Outside the U.S., Winfrey has become increasingly popular in the Arab world. The Wall Street Journal reported in 2007 that MBC 4, an Arab satellite channel, centered its entire programming around reruns of her show because it was drawing record numbers of female viewers in Saudi Arabia.

In 2008, The New York Times reported that The Oprah Winfrey Show, with Arabic subtitles, was broadcast twice each weekday on MBC 4. Winfrey's modest dress, combined with her attitude of triumph over adversity and abuse has caused some women in Saudi Arabia to idealize her.

CHAPTER 36.

Philanthropy

-Winfrey visits evacuees from New Orleans temporarily sheltered at the Reliant center in Houston following Hurricane Katrina.

In 2004, Winfrey became the first black person to rank among the 50 most generous Americans and she remained among the top 50 until 2010. By 2012 she had given away about $400 million to educational causes.

As of 2012, Winfrey had also given over 400 scholarships to Morehouse College in Atlanta, Georgia. Winfrey was the recipient of the first Bob Hope Humanitarian Award at the 2002 Emmy Awards for services to television and film. To celebrate two decades on national TV, and to thank her employees for their hard work, Winfrey took her staff and their families (1065 people in total) on vacation to Hawaii in the summer of 2006.

In 2013, Winfrey donated $12 million to the Smithsonian's National Museum of African American History and Culture. President Barack Obama awarded her the Presidential Medal of Freedom later that same year.

Oprah's Angel Network- In 1998, Winfrey created the Oprah's Angel Network, a charity that supported charitable projects and provided grants to nonprofit organizations around the world. Oprah's Angel Network raised more than $80,000,000 ($1 million of which was donated by Jon Bon Jovi). Winfrey personally covered all administrative costs associated with the charity, so 100% of all funds raised went to charity programs. The charity stopped accepting donations in May 2010 and was later dissolved.

In the wake of Hurricane Katrina, Oprah created the Oprah Angel Network Katrina registry which raised more than $11 million for relief efforts. Winfrey personally gave $10 million to the cause. Homes were built in Texas, Mississippi, Louisiana, Alabama before the one-year anniversary of Hurricanes Katrina and Rita.

South Africa.

Orah Winfrey Leadership Academy for Girls

In 2004, Winfrey and her team filmed an episode of her show, Oprah's Christmas Kindness , in which Winfrey travelled to South Africa to bring attention to the plight of young children affected by poverty and AIDS. During the 21-day trip, Winfrey and her crew visited schools and orphanages in poverty-stricken areas, and distributed Christmas presents to 50,000 children, with dolls for the girls and soccer balls for the boys, and school supplies.

Throughout the show, Winfrey appealed to viewers to donate money to Oprah's Angel Network for poor and AIDS-affected children in Africa. From that show alone, viewers around the world donated over $7,000,000. Winfrey invested $40 million and some of her time establishing the Oprah Winfrey Leadership Academy for Girls in Henley on Klip south of Johannesburg, South Africa. The school set over 22 acres, opened in January 2007 with an enrollment of 150 pupils (increasing to 450) and features state-of-the-art classrooms, computer and science laboratories, a library, theatre and beauty salon. Nelson Mandela praised Winfrey for overcoming her own disadvantaged youth to become a benefactor for others. Critics considered the school elitist and unnecessarily luxurious. Winfrey rejected the claims, saying: "If you are surrounded by beautiful things and wonderful teachers who inspire you, that beauty brings out the beauty in *you."Winfrey, who has no surviving biological children, described maternal feelings towards the girls at Oprah Winfrey Leadership Academy for Girls.Winfrey teaches a class at the school via satellite.*

CHAPTER 37.

Financial Transactions and Business Contracts -

Have you ever bought items at the store without a receipt? Have you ever had Bank accounts without a Statement of Account Showing your Account Balance to prove your spending habit.

Non Disclosure Agreement, Memorandum of Understanding and Contract Agreement as a proof of your business partnerships with your associates and you need an Articles of Association as a Bond with the party or parties you are involved with. This will help you keep things in perspective. Remind you of your Vision, your mission statement, the roles of the parties involved. Help you stay focused and you can have something to show incase things go wrong, or if you have to revisit or review the purpose and intent of the business. Never do business on just a handshake. Don't ever close the deal over a cup of coffee, a glass of wine or a lunch or dinner. Do the needful. Not just by smiling, taking pictures but by your contract papers and documents as proof. That is Wisdom and Its a smart thing to do. You will be protected at all levels.

The Money Smart are Generous Givers and they never lack.

Smart Mind-

I will be writings on this subject matter from my book Gold Mind- Sound Mind, You can never develop a smart mind or what I call the gold mind if you are not a reader or if You don't give to study. Readers are leaders and no one can lead effectively without a smart mind. You will have to manage people and resources. The rich hide things from others (The middle-class and the poor) by putting it all in a book. Because they know, that the problem with most people is reading. They use their knowledge power to their positive advantage. They know people find it hard to read the right things relevant to their lives. People will rather sit in front of the t.v set for hours than spend quality time reading to develop a smart mind. The rich know that people will rather waste time on irrelevant gossips on the internet than to read the right information relevant to their lives. Ignorance is never an excuse. I hereby say that the difference between every individual is knowledge, that is what you know. Knowledge is Light, Knowledge is power, Dare to know, Dare to Read, you will rub shoulders

with the high and mighty.
You can also get rich by selling premium products and exclusive Services.

Money Rule-

Rule #1- Money is a visitor just like any guest "meaning, your cash flow can increase or decrease, depending on economic factors like, inflation, deflation, demand, supply, emergencies, needs, unforeseen circumstances, Therefore, if you mismanage funds, you may be a victim of lack and wants. If you don't manage funds well, you will definitely get stranded at some point and may be forced to beg. You don't want to be a beggar, I am sure you want to be a giver. Let me let you know that the reason people beg is because they know there is a giver. Dare to be a giver and not a beggar. Begging is poverty, begging gives a negative impression and outlook of you. Rather ask!

Team Work-

Works, A single tree can never make a mighty forest,
You are the only one that best understands your idea, develop your skill to communicate it effectively. Your ability to communicate it effectively shows you believe, your passion, enthusiasm and motivation. Team work makes the Dream work.

Smart Vision-

No one embarks on a mission without a clear vision. I am sure you have visited different corporations either local or international, and you can see their Mission statement and corporate vision somewhere on the wall or on a piece of document. What are your vision for living? What is your financial vision in your lifetime, What is your future financial plans? In the next 1 year, 2 Years? 5 Years and 10 years from now? Time flies and before you know it, you are old. Ten years ago, you were probably in your twenties or thirties, now you are much older. Friends, just like that, another ten years is rolling by.
Look Smart- Be well dressed all the time. You don't have to wear the most expensive clothes or shoes, but look successful.
The Marketplace- The marketplace is not about who is right or wrong, but who is successful, Never see the glass as half empty, always see the glass as half full.Life is good and not miserable. develop that positive mental attitude.

OUR GLOBAL GOAL-

Our Dream is to end poverty in the World, and The Goal is to have at least 4 billion people read this Book, and Technology is our Strategy.
If this book has inspired you, be kind to buy one copy and give someone as a gift.

ABOUT THE AUTHOR-

Daniel "Goldmind" Born Adegbola Odebode Daniel.

Daniel Goldmind is the CEO/Founder of PIC. A company with Investments & Business Interests in Banking & Finance, Technology, Media & Advertising, Real Estate, Oil&Gas, Beverage, Agriculture,Telecoms, Mining and Consulting. He Is also a Financial Consultant, Investment Banker, Entrepreneur, Economist, Life Coach Trainer and Philanthropist. He hosts events all over the World as an International public speaker and Organizes Business Exhibitions for Large, Small and Medium Corporations. A solution Advisor in challenging areas of life. He Influences and Affect lives positively everywhere he goes. He delivers messages of transformation and practical applications through sharing experiences that empower people, because he believes "experience is the best teacher, but, doesn't have to be your experience, you can learn from other's experiences". As an accomplished author, speaker, actor, radio personality and film maker. Daniel has the instinct and intuition to connect with the audience by sharing mindset, methods and systems required to solve practical challenges in the Real World, Real Time.

For Booking Information Contact : Suite #A29, 220 31st Street, Miami Beach, FL. 33140-4103.
Or Call: +1-305-965-8291.
You can Pre-order his Books : MONEY BOOK: For Smart Kids; MONEY BOOK : For Teens & Young Adults. MONEY BOOK: For Leaders, The Government and Bread Winners; LOVE & SEX...The Truth About Romance & Finance In Relationships, Emotional Intelligence and The BELLAMAR (A True Life Story).

ISBN-13: 978-1502470133
ISBN-10: 1502470136